ANTIQUE CAR WRECKS

From Old Car's "WRECK OF THE WEEK" Photo Album

Edited by
John Gunnell

Published by:

krause publications

700 East State Street, Iola, WI 54990
Telephone: 715/445-2214

Library of Congress Catalog Number: 90-060581
ISBN: 0-87341-139-0
Printed in the United States of America

INTRODUCTION

The above photo relays the message of this book better than a full page of writing could. It tells us that the sight of a nice car, scrunched by a collision, can be used to make motorists drive more safely.

Professionals involved with highway safety programs have long recognized the educational value of photos showing wrecked automobiles. *The California Highway Patrolman* magazine has printed pictures of motor vehicle accidents, for more than 50 years, to promote safety consciousness.

Accident photos are also employed in the training of Emergency Medical Service personnel, fire-fighters and law enforcement officers. Safety researchers use pictures of wrecks to determine how and why accidents occur and what can be done to prevent them. Design engineers rely on photographic documentation to help them design more crashworthy cars.

Auto wrecks have been captured on film since at least 1903. Not long after that, the camera became an important tool for insurance companies. These firms found it convenient to document damage claims with photographs. Most pictures in this book were made for such a purpose.

Old Cars Weekly introduced its "Wreck of the Week" feature in 1984, as a means of promoting careful driving of antique autos. A safety message was included in most of the photo captions, at first, to make it clear that older cars using public highways must be driven extra carefully.

There are two reasons why hobby motoring requires special safety consciousness. The first has to do with the low-tech nature of vintage vehicles. Added to this is the lack of respect that some modern drivers exhibit towards old-fashioned cars traveling at a slower than ordinary pace.

As Abraham Lincoln might have predicted, the "Wreck of the Week" didn't please everyone. A handful of mail was received from people who missed the safety messages implied by the photos of wrecked old cars.

These people received courteous replies explaining that one of my interests, besides old cars, is highway safety. They were told that this is related to my work as a volunteer fireman, state-licensed ambulance attendant and Nationally Registered Emergency Medical Technician (NR-EMT). While undergoing education and training in these areas, the importance of "an ounce of prevention is worth a pound of cure" was impressed upon me again and again.

The "Wreck of the Week" proved to be an excellent way to get the attention of old car hobbyists and make them think about accident avoidance. Seeing the wreckage of cars like the ones they worked long hours to restore became a positive motivation to develop better driving habits.

Interest in the photo-feature grew rapidly. Pictures poured in from dozens — then hundreds — of people. Some were sent by hobbyists who had worked as insurance photographers years ago or old car buffs who collected such photos. Others were received from historians, museums, corporate archivists or people who had taken pictures of accidents they themselves endured.

Before very long, we had hundreds of photos. However, there were only 52 issues of *Old Cars Weekly* each year and it became impossible to use all the contributions. Many pictures had to be returned, rather than published, even though studies showed that most readers wanted to see them.

This book is the realization of a desire to expand the positive influences the "Wreck of the Week" feature has generated. Thanks to many photo contributors — particularly Frank Malatesta of Horseless Carriage Carriers in Paterson, N.J. and Randy Fleischhauer, of Mesa, Ariz. — the staff of *Old Cars Weekly* is happy to offer this photo album in the interest of safe hobby motoring and the continued preservation of antique automobiles.

Safety has taken on many different meanings throughout automotive history. Most of today's occupant protection devices were undreamed of in 1903, when this six horsepower DeDion Bouton was involved in an accident. (Photo courtesy National Motor Museum photographic library, Beaulieu, Hants, England)

Evolutions in Safety

By Edward A. Dellis

When gasoline was just pennies a gallon, men were jumping off running-boards to crash test cars. Today, sophisticated computer-aided techniques are used to test vehicles prior to tooling commitment. But the road to safety has been a long and hard one.

Safety has taken on many different meanings throughout the automobile's evolution. At first, some safety items we now take for granted were not even considered during the early stages of automobile development. For instance, despite their utility, headlights and windshields were not so obvious when the task at hand was simply to make the "thing" move with some semblance of reliability. In fact, it was not until the first known fatal car crash during the late 1800s that safety *per se* even became a design issue.

Evolutions in safety can be divided into two basic chronological categories: mechanical and electrical. In the early days the proliferation of mechanical devices sent many inventors to the U.S Patent Office. Cryptic safety items such as steering wheels (as opposed to tillers), doors, bumpers, fenders, hydraulic brakes, steel wheels with rubber tires

ROP (rollover protective structures), mechanical turn indicators, damping suspensions, padded interiors with "soft" control knobs, rear-view mirrors, speedometers and other gauges, and safety belts are just a few of these safety items that we tend to take for granted in today's automobile.

At first glance, early electrical safety enhancements appeared to be convenience items and only remotely related to safety. However, they did enhance overall vehicle safety and included filament-type headlamps, flashing turn signals, horns, multi-speed windshield wipers, electric starters, interior map lights, radios, cruise controls, air conditioner-type defrosters, and improved instrumentation — among others.

Milestones in the evolution of safety

Headlights represent a type of electrical equipment which contributed to highway safety. This 1926 Chevrolet truck, photographed at a GM proving grounds, is being used to test safety under wet driving conditions.

"*you buy ém we`ll fly ém!*"

R.R.Wilkinsons

DEFENSE BONDS STAMPS

THE MORE BONDS YOU BUY—THE MORE PLANES WILL FLY

Seat belts can be traced back to aviation, where they were first used to keep pilots from falling out of inverted planes. Dr. John P. Stapp's volunteer test work helped develop the lap and shoulder harness restraint system first used in World War II aircraft.

are rarely recognized as such at their inception. Even anti-lock brake systems seem to have taken a decade to become viable commercially in the U.S. But safety is still a maturing industry and it has made vast progress along the way.

Seat belts

Seat belt use can be traced back to early aviation when it was thought that the belts were there only to keep pilots from separating form their planes during inverted flight. Circa 1935, Hugh DeHaven, an engineer and World War I fighter pilot, who barely survived a plane crash wearing only a lap belt, became interested in human survival that involved falls from 15-50 miles. His efforts led to the establishment of a crash injury reasearch program at Cornell University Medical Collge that, today, operates as Calspan Field Services.

The three-point safety belt system was the brainchild of Dr. Bertil Aldman, a Swedish anesthesiologist, and Nils Bohlin, a safety engineer from the Volvo Automobile Co. Since the belt's introduction into the firm's automobiles in 1959, crash data indicated that the belts were effective in preventing fatal accidents below 96 km/h, while unrestrained occupants died in vehicles that traveled less than 19 km/h prior to impact.

Just about when customers were demanding big-bore V8s and not safety items, the National Highway Safety Bureau was initiated and headed up by Dr. William Haddon, Jr.; the year was 1966. Now it is called the National Highway Traffic and Safety Administration (NHTSA). During his stay with the organization, Dr. Haddon wrote the Federal Motor Vehicle Safety Standards (FMVSS) which established a

ness. Bela Barenyi of Daimler-Benz realized the need to design for vehicular energy absorption, a principle of which the public is still largely ignorant. The principle was taken a step further and moved to the vehicle's interior in which the second impact — actually Hugh DeHaven's concept whereby the occupant strikes the interior upon crash ride-down — is reduced by the use of energy absorbing materials on contact surfaces.

Time and distance are the two factors that affect the energy transferred to the occupants during a crash. The concept is to let the vehicle absorb as much of the crash energy as possible by crushing while transfering as little as possible to the occupants contained in a rigid passenger compartement. The process of absorbing crash energy is called "ride-down."

Early race car accidents provided a test bed for future safety enhancements of production vehicles. This 1933 wreck occurred when Lester Spangler's car struck a wall, rolled along the top of it and crossed a short stretch.

At about the same time, jet propulsion was finding its way into aviation. Dr. John P. Stapp, a U.S. Army Air Force physician, volunteered for and survived a 49 g. deceleration test in an effort to determine the human tolerance for deceleration. His efforts provided valuable information for the lap and shoulder harness restraint systems used in WW II aircraft, American space exploration, and automobiles. In 1956, the first Stapp Car Crash Conference was held and, even today, is regarded as a prestigious forum for research in vehicle design, human injury tolerance, and injury control.

minimum safety code which all vehicles sold in the U.S. must meet. The code stands today and covers design criteria starting with the FMVSS 100s (pre-crash), on to the 200s (crash), and finishes with the 300s (post-crash) requirements. But it was the Swedish data regarding crash survivability of occupants in Volvos equipped with lap and shoulder belts that led to its requirement in the FMVSS code in 1968.

Energy absorption

The 1953 Mercedes 180 was designed with a patented feature that paved the way for improved vehicle crash-worthi-

Vehicular energy absorption has the benefit of extended time and distance in which to perform its task. However, the second impact does not share the advantagous long ride-down path of the first impact, which often includes a hood and undercarriage. Instead, the crush distance of the second impact is limited to the occupant's salient facial features and displacement of the interior's impacted material. The time factor is reduced by one order in magnitude during a typical head-on 56 km/h crash into a tree: 100 ms. versus 10 ms., primary versus secondary impacts, respectively. Crush distance shares the

In the early 1950s, delivering new cars was basically an uncomplicated task. Recently, companies such as Porsche have launched programs in which buyers of specific models are being sent to advanced driving schools.

same reduction: 50-85 cm. versus typically a few centimeters, primary versus secondary impacts, respectively.

Since the increase of either variable results in reductions of impact through improved ride-down, collapsible steering columns, and safety glass with 75 percent peripheral retention evolved to aid impact reduction by decreasing occupant g. load.

The third impact

There is a third impact that is recently getting special attention. It involves the body's organs as they strike its skeletal structure. Of particular interest is the brain skull combination.

Previously, even the best dummies in the industry only addressed accelerations at one point on the spine. This same simple dummy can be used for the current aceleration-only federal standard.

But in the 1960s, General Motors Research (GMR) labs, together with Current Product Engineering Safety Research and Development, established the Theory of Compression Criterion to predict injury impact using a Hybrid III dummy. This dummy measured the compression between the front and rear surfaces of the body cavity. The theory was derived by varying the amounts of compression, while holding the velocity of impact within a narrow range. Therefore, velocity essentially remained constant.

In 1981, Dr. David C. Viano and Dr. Ian V. Lau of GM extended compression criterion with a hypothesis of their own. An outgrowth of their work was the Viscous Criterion which can be used to predict injuries to organs such as liver, spleen, heart, and other soft tissues including the central nervous system.

Whereas the earlier compression criterion study found that compression determined injury in an impact when velocity was controlled, the new study

Evolutions in auto safety can be divided into two basic categories. Mechanical devices, such as the equipment being tested here at a GM proving grounds, helped bring many safety advances.

The 1948 Tucker was one of the first cars to feature a "crash compartment" for passengers.

found that velocity determined injury when compression was controlled. Instantaneous compression is multiplied by deformation velocity to obtain a viscous injury response as a function of time. They found that an impact of 4400 kg.n 1/500 second is survivable. The discovery that human tissue is essentially time-strain dependent has led to a rethinking in the way the second impact ride-down is handled. This evolution in injury mechanisms and human tolerance guided the development of Inland Division's self-aligning steering wheel.

Recent work at GMR labs provided new three-dimensional acceleration and force measurements using a Hybrid III, neck load cell dummy. Finally, translational head acceleration can be addressed with rotational acceleration. This, in combination with high-speed data acquisition, is allowing new input for a finite element model used to interpret brain injury risks.

Statistics can direct real-world safety design. Dr. Leonard Evans, principal research scientist for GM had developed a double pair comparison. The method uses fatal crash data to determine how certain characteristics of vehicle occupants will affect their probability of death if they are involved in an automobile accident. As applied to rear seat safety belts, the double pair comparison revealed that there is an 18 percent reduction in fatality risk with lap-belt-only application (as opposed to unbelted application), but a significant improvement could be gained by the use of lap-shoulder belts. This has led to GM's decision to introduce lap-shoulder belts as standard equipment in the outboard rear seating positions. Similar

treatment to driver and front seat passengers wearing lap-shoulder belts revealed a 43 percent reduction in fatalities without otherwise changing their behavior.

Today's safety arena

With today's highly competitive, fast-paced market driven by customer needs and wants, care must be exercised not to compromise the integrity of the vehicle's safety design for the customer's "ignorant comfort."

Quality function deployment allows screened collection of items that can be called customer requirements. Perhaps one item on that wish list might read: "comfortable, easy-to-use safety belt." A brainstorming session on such a requirement can unleash a whirlwind of creativity that eventually leads to an improved safety environment for occupants.

On the other hand, real world misapplications of these ingenious devices might lead to compromises in overall safety by the devices' misuse or non-use. The disappearance of customer-inspired seat belt comfort clips and windowshade-type ratchet retractors (which allowed users to maintain slack in the shoulder portion of three-point belts, while being otherwise securely fastened) is testimony to the realization that the customer is *not* always right when it comes to safety.

The next evolution in safety will challenge engineers with a liability situation that is face-to-face with a market-inspired, customer-driven design methodology. Even fleet testing of new safety devices is now virtually impossible. So far, the situation has essentially forced manufacturers to become excessively cautious while making design concessions on perfectly operational hardware whose original design concept was sound. Due care must be taken in the design of safety items, but the fear of a possible lawsuit should not preclude the creativity that might ultimately lead to a safer occupant environment.

Accident avoidance

Accident avoidance appears to be the next plateau on the auto-safety horizon. GM's Project Trilby is addressing

The safety-conscious 1948 Tucker featured a "cyclops" headlamp which turned in the direction in which the car was steered.

The interior of this 1956 Ford illustrates the optional "Lifeguard" safety equipment package introduced that year.

With the advent of electronics "smart" safety will be possible. Already passive belts, anti-lock braking systems, and adaptive hardware are products of improved electronics. Mercedes-Benz now has a pop-up roll bar and self-tightening seat belt retractors. Airbags are already standard on every Chryler passenger car manufactured in the U.S., 13 upscale GM models, and eight Ford models.

With the proposed Dynamic Side Impact Test (FMVSS 214) undergoing evaluation to simulate better real-world situations, side impact protection is receiving special attention. Work at GM carefully analyzes the type of injuries sustained in these impacts and suggests alternate designs that relocate inner door hardware out of harm's way, while placing energy absorbing padding in its place.

2000 and beyond. . .

The accident avoidance frontier coupled with advanced electronics should pit proximity sensing together with on-board navigational aids and vision enhancement to provide improved safety. It might not be too far off before radio interruptions will warn drivers of incipient red-light running. And, before we even know it, Big Brother might be actually watching out for our safety.

*Information for this article was provided by **Dr. David C. Viano, Ph.D.**, General Motors Research Laboratories; an article and photograps by **Dr. John D. States, M.D.**, and proceedings from the Symposium on Motor Vehicle Injuries both published by The New York Academy of Medicine; **Dr. Jerry Barancik Sc.D.**, Brookhaven National Laboratory, Injury Prevention and Analysis Group; and **Bert Smith**, Chrysler Motors Corp. The article is reprinted, with permission, from **AUTOMOTIVE ENGINEERING** magazine, January 1990. Society of Automotive Engineers, Inc.*

human factors issues as an integral part of the vehicle design process. This includes detailed studies of how drivers do their jobs. Driving simulators and camera-equipped cars are allowing evaluation of various in-vehicle controls, displays, and warning systems to aid drivers.

Improved driver education will help to raise the level of awareness for tomorrow's drivers. There is a concern that the proliferation of safety devices might lull drivers into a false sense of security by their heavy reliance upon them. Even today, drivers must realize that anti-lock braking systems are not panaceas for accident avoidance. One researcher astutely observed tht ABS might only move the accident from the front end of the vehicle to the rear end. This would make an otherwise bullet vehicle into a target vehicle.

In the near future, an awareness of the limitations of newly purchased state-of-the-art hardware will be necessary so that drivers do not attempt to deny the laws of physics with their vehicles. A rethinking of vehicle delivery to customers at the dealership level could prevent unexpected performance from contributing to accidents. Already evidence of this is happening as manufacturers such as Porsche are sending customers to advanced driving schools with the purchase of vehicles, while others such as GM and Ford are sending their corporate executives.

Some drivers are lucky...others are smart!

This advertisement for Goodyear "Lifeguard" tires depicted an accident caused by a blow-out. It sent the car being towed away skidding off the road into a ditch. The other car also had a blow-out, but the Lifeguard tire — with two air chambers — allowed it to come to a gradual halt due to the air in the inner chamber. Tire improvements, over the years, have been one of the highlights of automotive safety.

Highlights of Automotive Safety

In 1894, W. W. Austin of Lowell, Mass., was killed at the Charles River Race track in Boston while testing a steam car he had built. Austin's steamer collided with a similar machine being operated on the track and he was thrown to his death. This has been recorded as probably the first two-car collision in American history.

Accidents relating to the use of early self-propelled vehicles soon prompted those responsible for designing and building cars to think about the safety of motorists. Eventually this led to the creation of what we now call safety equipment.

When you think of automotive safety devices what features come to your mind? Perhaps you are picturing lights, horns, bumpers; or you could be envisioning seat belts, padded dashboards and laminated safety glass. You see, there are actually two basic types of safety equipment and one kind is older than the other.

The first safety features that appeared on cars were designed chiefly by mechanical engineers who applied their knowledge to the problem of minimizing driving hazards. Many years later the field of human engineering would evolve, bringing with it new approaches to motoring safety.

The first safety devices to appear on motor cars were designed chiefly to help avoid accidents. They were introduced in what is known as the "Builder Period" — that is, the years in which they very first cars were made. More safety innovations came during the "Production Period," which lasted from 1908 to 1914. During World War I, automotive technology screeched to a halt and it wasn't until the "Owner Period" that more safety advances were made. This lasted from 1920 to about 1939 and was followed by the "Extra Equipment Era," in which safety got mainly "lip service." It wasn't until 1948 that the first true safety car appeared and marked the beginning of the "Human Engineering Period," which we are still in today.

It's interesting to look back at all these periods and the changes that took place in each one, because doing this shows very clearly that the machines we are driving now are really the safest

there ever were. Such a backward glance will lead us to just one conclusion — and we'll see what this is in a while. First, let's see how the improvements came one by one.

The Builder Period

One of the first pieces of safety equipment to appear on automobiles was the simple squeeze-type horn. Such a device was optional equipment on the Curved Dash Oldsmobile of 1901. In the old days beeping your horn was not legally recognized as a claim to the right of way. In most localities the rules of the road had been established long before the automobile appeared. Motor cars had to abide by the same ordinances and regulations as the more common horse drawn vehicle. Of course, accidents don't usually happen when the rules are being followed. Mishaps always seem to take place when two drivers both think they're in the right. So drivers started equipping cars with horns to let others know when they thought the law was on their side. That way, everyone within earshot at least knew what they were thinking.

Shock absorbers appeared as early as 1904. These units are the type used on 1929 Oaklands.

One of the first safety devices was the bulb horn. One is shown here, mounted on the tiller of a Curved Dash Oldsmobile in the Imperial Palace Auto Collection.

In 1900, the first year of the "Builder Period," The R.E. Dietz Co. — a lamp-making concern — announced a line of specially-made automobile lights. These were kerosene-burning types, much the same as those used earlier on wagons. There were various types specially-designed as headlights, taillamps and side lights. In 1902, Gray & Davis Lamps Co., of Amesbury, Mass., advertised special lamp for steam driven automobiles. Then, in 1904, the automotive lighting industry was greatly advanced by the introduction of headlights powered by acetylene gas dissolved in acetone stored in a tank. This was called the Prest-O-Lite system and had been developed by James Allison and Carl G. Fisher, based on Eugene Bournonville's ideas. The Prest-O-Lite system was used on many cars until the mid-teens.

The necessity for official regulation of motor vehicle speeds began in 1901, with the states of New York and Connecticut passing laws governing top speeds. Other states soon followed their example. In 1902, for example, the city of Minneapolis arrested one Thomas H. Shevlin and fined him $10 for exceeding the 10 mph speed limit in his new French car. Like other speeders would argue later, Shevlin insisted that his car could not go any slower.

By the end of 1905, the first speedometer was being developed so people would know how fast their cars were traveling. The introduction of the tachometer followed shortly thereafter. In reality, both of these instruments added to the safety of the roads.

A number of other safety features were soon to come along as well. The steering wheel was first seen in in 1900 and the original adjustable version was

an innovation of 1903. Wooden wheels with double-tubed tires came on the market in 1901 and the pneumatic tire proved to make driving safer, too. In 1904, France made a test on the first anti-skid chains and, in America, brands such as Parsons and Weed chains were soon seen on many cars

used in the mud or snow. In the same year, E.V. Hartford, the father of the shock absorber movement, began merchandising the Trauffault-Hartford type.

Windshields were also introduced in 1904 to protect early drivers from dirt, dust and flying objects. By 1905, three different makes of cars at the Chicago Automobile Show sported accessory windshields. The Gabriel Tubular Horn was another device first seen that season. All of these safety devices were sold as extra-cost optional equipment.

Headlamps and parking lamps are safety devices, but the hood ornament on this Packard doesn't look very safe. (Bill Ballas photo)

The Model T Ford was a major factor in the "Production Period" of automotive history, which brought us more safety equipment. The folding windshield on this car was one of them.

Bumpers became a common accessory for automobiles in the early 1920s. This Kissel Gold Bug features a massive, triple-bar unit.

The Production Period

From 1908 to about 1914 the next period, stressing mass production, unfolded. The new Ford Model T, announced in October 1908, saw a production run of 20,000 units — a previously unimaginable total. A year later the Indianapolis Motor Speedway opened its doors and would soon become a competitive test bed for many industry ideas, including some concerned with safety.

The fully-equipped automobile was the big news of 1910 and the new cars that year looked quite a bit different from earlier models. In terms of styling, it was the "torpedo body" that aroused great interest, but safety, too, was greatly advanced. And as many new safety features were now considered regular equipment.

The pioneer of the fully-equipped model was the new car offered by Ralph Owens, which bore his name on the radiator. Included in the vast aray of standard equipment were windshields, electric horns, electric-acetylene lighting and electric side lights and taillights. In Europe that same year, Isotta marked the first production model to offer four-wheel brakes. When these were later introduced in the United States, several manufacturers would wage a publicity campaign against them as being unsafe. This effort did not last long, however, and this feature soon became standard on all cars.

In the last few years of this period electric lighting was almost universally adopted in the auto industry. The first types of rearview mirrors appeared about 1911. They were produced by the Kales Stamping Co., of Detroit, and were called "hindview mirrors." In 1913, Pierce-Arrow started a long-standing tradition of placing headlamps on the front fenders to make sure the beams would do more good for motorists traveling by night.

The Owner Period

Cars didn't change very much from 1914 to the early 1920s, due to the intervention of war in Europe. When the industry got the assembly lines rolling again, safety took a back seat to other considerations. However, the mighty Duesenberg did get American's first four-wheel brakes in 1921. Bumpers were another safety device that became popular at this point. The first bumpers appeared as early as 1904, but their function was chiefly ornamental then. In 1909, an attempt at forming an association of bumper manufacturers was made, but patent problems led to the quick dissolution of the group. It would be almost ten years before the Biflex type of wide faced bumpers, with two or three parallel bars, came into wide acceptance.

Automatic windshield wipers also became a common feature on cars after WWI. This was because the coupe and sedan were gaining wide popularity. With earlier, open-bodied cars drivers would simply lean out with a rag to clean windshields. A second way to solve the problem was to have a folding windshield where the top glass panel could be adjusted to a horizontal positon. This allowed full visibility in the rain, though drivers would get a bit wet. The first windshield wipers were operated by hand, but the introduction of the vacuum-operated automatic type was a real improvement. In 1924, the American Bosch Magneto Corp., of Springfield, Mass., started selling electric wipers and these cost $9.50. They could also be fitted with a tandem lingage so that two or even three wipers would sweep across the glass.

New safety door locks were seen in 1922, and by 1925 Nash was ready to release four-wheel brakes as standard on then popular-priced cars. By the time Ford's famous Model A came along in 1927-28, even this low priced new car had four-wheel brakes, electric wipers and Triplex shatterproof glass.

The Extra-Equipment Era

The Model A, like other cars made in the late 1920s, was a great value for the money. For example, the Sport Coupe, at $550, had a long list of features that greatly improved styling, safety and comfort. The Great Depression, however, would devastate the economics of the auto industry and bring significant changes in merchandising policies. Within a few years, the lowest priced models sold by many manufacturers would carry a minimum of equipment. Additional features were now being offered as accessories which added to the base factory price of the car. Unfortunately, American buyers were less likely to spend extra money on safety than on special trim or performance features.

During these year a lot of "lip service" was given to the idea of safety, but few real advances were made. There were Saf-T seat cushions, Saf-T Flex steering

Among unusual safety accessories, available in the 1930s, were wide "Jumbo" balloon tires. They were patterned after aircraft tire designs. One type is seen here on a Hupmobile coach. (Goodyear Tire Co. photo)

wheels and Saf-T brakes. But, in reality, there was really very little in the way of new innovations. There were technical improvements that made all cars a bit safer, but most were simply refinements of old ideas. There was truly a lack of real creativity as far as human engineering went. The word "safety" was being used to sell more cars, but the impression of increased safety was a false one. Death rates from accidents started to climb at an alarming rate.

Human Engineering Era

In the midst of this situation, the first real safety car evolved at the end of World War II. Unfortunately the Tucker Automobile barely got into production, when a number of factors ended the pioneering project almost before it began. Just slightly over 50 of these cars were ever built prior to the firm's collapse.

When Preston Tucker first announced his plans to build a totally new kind of automobile, he was quick to advise the public that it would be the safest car ever made. The Tucker had symmetrically-balanced steering and a fully independent suspension. Safe-T-Plate glass was used in all of the car's windows and the windshield was made to pop out in case of an accident. A heavy crash pad surrounded the entire passenger compartment. The dashboard and doors had no protruding knobs or handles. The door latches were of a flush-fitting type, with no protrusions. A soft, padded bulkhead protected passengers against bumping their heads.

Large, strong and attractive full-width bumpers were used. They offered superior impact protection. The undercarriage was designed in such a way that no components — such as pipes, levers and rods — ran below the floorboards below the passenger compartment.

All undercarriage bolts on the Tucker were attached with large Allen bolts, according to aircraft construction practice. A unitized body was used, along with a sturdy frame having 10 exceptionally rigid crossmembers. A "cyclops" central headlight was used. It turned in whatever direction the car was steered.

All instruments were designed to avoid reflections at night and glare during the day. The doors opened into the roof, to keep passengers from hitting their heads when entering or getting out. The front driving cockpit was designed as a crash cellar. The car even had standard seat belts at first, though these were later abandoned because it was felt they would give the impression of an unsafe machine. However, the real character of the Tucker was one of total safety. In fact, many of its advanced features would later become mandatory safety devices on all American cars. The Tucker was the first car to enter production with human engineering as a prime consideration in its design.

Soon after World War II ended, those who had worked in the relatively new fields of human engineering and industrial design found work in the auto industry. Their influence was first found in the products of smaller manu-

factuers, such as Studebaker, Willys and Kaiser-Frazer. The large automakers were so busy turning strong profits that safety design took a back seat again. Surprisingly, it was Chrysler — one of the most conservative large manufacturers - who first considered offering seat belts as an accessory. By 1950, you could also order a padded dashboard in some Chrysler models.

However, it was the Ford Motor Co. that made a most significant safety advance in 1956, with an attempt to merchandise real safety features. That year both Ford and Mercury models were available with a wide selection of safety equipment hailed as "Lifeguard" accessories. These included padded dashboards, padded inside sun visors, improved door locks, safety seat belts, double-swivel rearview mirrors and deep-dish steering wheels. These features were fully backed up with a unique advertising campaign highlighting the "Lifeguard" theme. By the end of the year, the failure of this expensive promotion proved it was next to impossible to sell the public on the importance of safety in automotive design.

Ford's failure in selling safety features as accessories merely emphasized the fact that highway slaughter would continue unless something drastic was done on another level. Concerned parties in various places, including government, were getting the message loud and clear. The only way to cut down America's accident toll would be to make automotive safety equipment mandatory.

Thus, in 1966, President Lyndon Johnson's administration enacted the Highway Safety Act of 1966. This was a landmark piece of federal legislation that gave Washington sweeping powers over the design of American cars. The act specified a number of mandatory safety standards that were to become effective in the 1968 model year. In addition, the government was able to convince Detroit to add six standard safety features to all 1966 domestic cars. These were: padded instrument panels, padded sun visors, seat belts, backup lights, left-hand outside mirrors and windshield washers. Two years later, approximately 14 other features found on all cars today were made mandatory.

This then brings us to the conclusion we spoke of earlier. The cars we drive today are the safest ever built cannot be denied. And as users of American highways and roads, we have a responsibility to operate those machines as carefully and wisely as possible. Afterall, it has taken over 80 years of long, hard striving for perfection to produce the modern and safe automobile.

(This article is reprinted with permission from The California Highway Patrolman, a magazine published by The Association of California Highway Patrolmen).

This is a front view of a 1913 or 1914 Overland with license plates indicating that it was wrecked in 1919 in New Jersey. Side with bent fender and broken wheel shows frame intact, while right-hand frame (but not fender) is badly bent. Note horse-drawn vehicle in background. "Horse sense" comes in handy when you're driving antique automobiles. (Frank Malatesta Collection).

This wreck inflicted heavy damage to the Model T Ford on the right. The unidentified large touring car on the left appears repairable. Notice the broom propped against the rear wheel, which someone used to sweep debris. "This proves that accidents did happen years ago," wrote Allister Fame, general manager of the Classic Car Museum of Victoria, B.C., who sent the photo. Scenes like this should inspire old car hobbyists to drive their antique autos safely.

Damage to rear fender and runningboard of this Model T Ford Couplet is relatively light, but notice the bullet hole in rear of the body. Car appears to date to 1923-1924, but photo was snapped Sept. 13, 1930 and license plates are of 1930 issue. Don't "spare" safety when touring in your T. (Frank Malatesta Collection)

This large touring car was involved in a bad accident on Jan. 30, 1929. Judging from the headlights, it could be a Buick. Wood spoke artillery wheels didn't hold up well in heavy impacts. The snow on the ground and the buttoned-up side curtains were winter driving hazards. (Frank Malatesta Collection)

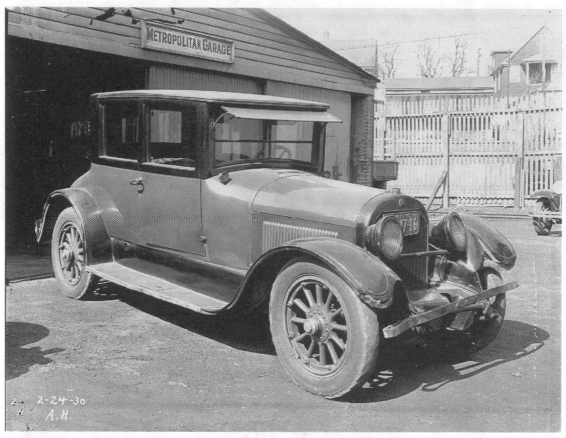

This 1922-1923 Cadillac coupe suffered relatively minor damage in a fender-bender. Photo was snapped Feb. 24, 1930 and the car has current New York license plates. Car was taken to the Metropolitan Garage for repairs. Take it easy in your Cadillac! (Frank Malatesta Collection)

A family in period garb views the remains of a 1920s sedan which was involved in a heavy collision. Jeff Gillis, of the Durant Family Registry provided this picture of the car, beside an old filling station, to help promote safe driving of the antique cars he loves.

A front end impact re-shaped the face of this Model T Ford coupe in a Sept. 1929 accident. You can really appreciate shatterproof glass when you look at the passenger side of the windshield on this car. Restore your antiques with safety glass! (Frank Malatesta Collection)

Lessons learned from racing accidents have contributed greatly to the development of safer passenger cars. This accident took place during an early road race. It shows bystanders scurrying away from an out of control race car. Winning takes a back seat to safety when it comes to the "human race!"

It's obviously no accident that the next wreck you'll see in this book was captured on film. The late-1920s touring car seen here was used by General Tire Co. in a test of how blow-out proof tires performed during collisions. That "smashing" looking fellow in the leather helmet (with a tie no less) is a professional test driver.

Test car impacts a brick barrier, causing forward momentum of driver, who wisely avoided sitting directly behind steering column. Blow-out proof ties seem to have held up well. This General Tire Co. photo should make you think about why it took more than 25 years before automakers started offering seat belts in their products.

It's doubtful that this car made it to the auto show advertised on wall poster. The 1923 Rickenbacker sedan — named after the World War I flying ace who later purchased the Indianapolis Motor Speedway — needs some fender repairs and a headlight re-aimed. Put your hat-in-the-ring for old car safety. (Frank Malatesta Collection)

The tire that was on the splintered front wheel of this Studebaker sits on the front seat. There is a 1923 license plate hanging from the headlamp tie-bar. Notice the rear view mirror added to the left front fender and the period bicycle behind the car. This scene clearly demonstrates the need to take extra care when driving through intersections.

Rare 1925 Peerless was the unfortunate victim of careless driving habits. Look at how the left end of bumper has been pushed right into the side of the tire. This photo was snapped Aug. 5, 1930. Preserve those rare cars — drive carefully. (Frank Malatesta Collection)

This photo was submitted as evidence (exhibit no. 81) in a Jan. 8, 1924 case heard in the Essex County (N.J.) Court of Common Pleas. The car with its front against the curb is a 1922 or 1923 Studebaker sedan that was in very nice condition before it met the Model T Ford center door sedan at an intersection. Remember not to cut corners where it comes to safe driving!

New Jersey License plate for this 1925 Chevy was issued in 1930. However, the photo was taken Jan. 27, 1931, so the car may have sat awhile. Notice the bent up radiator grille. Those accessory wind wings aren't very aerodynamic. For safety, keep your antique auto registrations up-to-date. (Frank Malatesta Collection)

This truck looks like a "slant windshield" model following accident which took place May 2, 1924. It appears to have a mechanically operated stake bed and damage to runningboard and rear fender. Remember, we all have a stake in the safe operation of vintage vehicles. (Frank Malatesta Collection)

Lee Webber, of Santa Rosa, Calif., sent in this photo — plaintiff's exhibit no. 1 — from the files of a 1925 San Francisco lawsuit. Note the chains attached to both frame horns, which were used to tow the wreck to a storage and repair garage. Remember that careful driving is an important link in the auto safety chain!

Tires on this 1925-1926 Model T are real "baldies." The accident which damaged the hood and left front fender also broke the wood rimmed steering wheel. Photo dates from Sept. 5, 1933, when this Ford had little value. Steer your antique auto on the road to safer driving. (Frank Malatesta Collection)

Oval rear window was a feature of the now-very-collectible Model T center door sedan. Chances are good that this example never made it into a collector's hands. Accidents always seem to draw a crowd, but some onlookers — like the lad near the tree on the left — seem unimpressed by the wreck. Hopefully, the smash up made more of a safe driving impression on some of the other folks.

Although it was forcibly removed, the bumper from this little tourer seems to have done a good job of protecting the vehicle from heavy accident damage. It looks like a 1925-1924 Chevy, but we can't be definitely sure. (Frank Malatesta Collection)

Motorcycles were among the many types of antique vehicles which were involved in highway accidents. This early Harley-Davidson had a real rear fender-bender. Photo was taken June 14, 1930, but the vintage of the "bike" is a mystery. (Frank Malatesta Collection)

A 1924-1925 Ford Model T coupe wound up in a salvage yard after a June 1927 accident twisted it beyond repair. There aren't many straight panels left on the poor little "flivver." Safe-T suits the "T" to a tee! (Frank Malatesta Collection)

We doubt that minor dings on right front fender put this 1925 Buick out of commission for very long. It was photographed on May 16, 1934. Bald tires were a real safety problem in the 1930s. Put good tires on your old car. (Frank Malatesta Collection)

Photo shows an old Reo produce truck that was wrecked during May of 1936. The left front fender is twisted like a roller coaster. Arden Farm Products, Inc., operated the commercial vehicle in New Jersey, but the year of manufacture is unknown. (Frank Malatesta Collection)

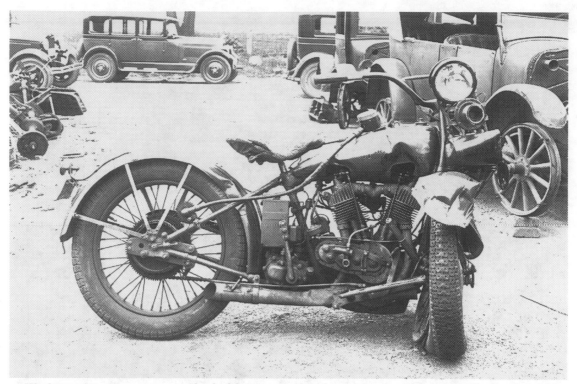

We haven't seen many wrecked old motorcycles, but this photo shows a Harley-Davidson that wound up in a scrapyard after a crash that occurred in the late 1920s. Ride your antique bikes extra-safely! (Frank Malatesta Collection)

A driver for the Ridgewood-Midland Park Washing Co., of Ridgewood, N.J., may have had some explaining to do, after banging-up the company's International delivery van on Dec. 29, 1928. The truck looks like it is almost new — or was until the accident took place. Drive your antique truck safely! (Frank Malatesta Collection)

Circa-1924 Packard had its right front fender rumpled in an accident during April 1926. There's some heavy front end damage, too. Note the through-the-windshield Clymer spot-lamp and the winterfront. Ask the man who owns one — Packards love safe driving! (Frank Malatesta Collection)

Brougham Sedan model with overhanging roof visor, was a midyear 1925 introduction from Hudson. This example lasted less than two years, before it was badly wrecked. There is another Hudson in the garage in front of car. Drive your Hudsons safely at all times. (Frank Malatesta Collection)

Close-up photo shows a 1925 Star Landau Sedan damaged in a 1929 accident. Accessory stoplamp obviously wasn't heeded by owner of second car involved in this crash. Note shades in rear and rear quarter windows. Be a "star" in the antique car safe-driving movement by using extra care on the road. (Frank Malatesta Collection)

Here's one way (not recommended) to make a four-door into a two-door. Front tire of 1936 Cadillac might have been hard to turn with fender smashed down on it. The photo taken on Christmas Eve in 1935 gives a good view of the car's jump seat. Don't close the door on safety when you're touring! (Frank Malatesta Collection)

Disk wheels were optional on 1926-1927 Pontiacs. Notice the tube from rear tire hanging out of wheel rim. This Landau Sedan body style was introduced in the fall of 1926, so car was about five years old when it crashed. When touring in your oldtime car, make sure you have good tubes in the tires. (Frank Malatesta Collection)

Just a little restoration work would turn this 1925 Buick sedan into a real show winner. Even this "better built" motorcar rode around a bald tires during the depression. Great-looking Duco finish, introduced in 1925, still shines after 12 years. Set a shining safety example when you drive your old car. (Frank Malatesta Collection)

Oakland Motor Car Co.'s slogan was "as sturdy as the oak," but this Oakland didn't look to sturdy when photographed on Feb. 4, 1930. It's a 1926 Landau sedan. Don't make a smash in the hobby . . . drive your Oakland safely. (Frank Malatesta Collection)

This poor 1926-1927 Pontiac wouldn't even make a real good parts car after devastating wreck that occurred in May, 1931. Indian hood mascot seems to have "turned other cheek" after car was hit by something big and heavy. Keep your eyes on the road ahead when you go out for an antique car ride. (Frank Malatesta Collection)

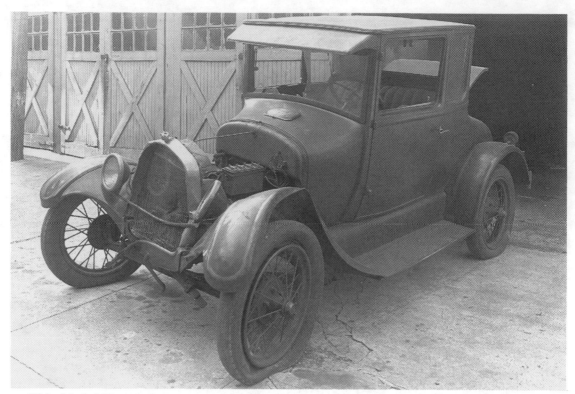

This Model T was about two years old when insurance company photographer took this picture on Sept. 23, 1929. Frontal impact had enough shock to open rear deck lid. Note identification marks chalked on radiator. Put the lid on unsafe driving; use care when you hit the road. (Frank Malatesta Collection)

Chains used to tow this 1927 Buick Sport Coupe away from accident scene are still attached to rear bumper. Only 7,178 of these cars were built for the U.S. market. This one was wrecked on March 6, 1933. Drive your Buick safely. (Frank Malatesta Collection)

This 1926-1927 Ford Model T roadster wound up against a utility pole, following an accident which took place in a Wisconsin city. The Goodyear Balloon spare tire looks like it is brand new. Take extra care when driving antique autos in a city. (Peter F. Zierden)

Following a minor front end collision, this 1926 Jewett Six "New Day" coach wound up with a bent bumper, banged-up fenders and mis-aimed headlamps. This was the only Jewett model to feature the narrow windshield corner posts. The last Jewetts were built in Sept. 1926, as 1927 models. The name was changed to Paige in Jan. 1927. (Peter F. Zierden)

Packard lovers will breathe a sigh of relief when they see that this 1927 model has only minor damage to its right front fender. License plate and April 9, 1936 date on photo indicate when this car was hit. "Ask the man who owns one" about what good sense it makes to drive a Packard safely. (Frank Malatesta Collection)

This 1930 Packard sedan wound up on its roof in the middle of a railroad track after a bad accident. It appears the car may have plunged from the roadway above, where a crowd of onlookers has gathered. Amazingly, if that's the case, it is not totally flattened.

A bent bumper and dinged-up front fender were among the damage this 1927 Studebaker incurred during an accident which occurred in Oct. 1933. Drive your "Studie" with a steady hand! (Frank Malatesta Collection)

Not much has changed in the 60 years since this 1927 Willys Model 93-A sedan was in a fender-bender. Shop signs announce "all parts and labor strictly cash" and "if not on business, keep out." Notice the stamped tin wall. Put your stamp of approval on safe hobby driving! (Frank Malatesta Collection)

Something seems to have fallen on the top surface of the rear deck lid of this 1927 Willis St. Clair roadster, causing minor damage. This Oct. 9, 1929 photo shows the car had lots of "goodies" to enhance its sporty looks. Safe driving is good for the entire antique car hobby! (Frank Malatesta Collection)

Styling of this type was seen on 1931-1932 Diamond Reo trucks. Early and later models did not have vent doors in their hoods. Judging by the 1935-1936 Wisconsin license plate, this damage occurred when it was four to five years old. "Dump" some safety into the antique truck hobby; drive carefully. (Peter F. Zierden)

Whatever hit the doors of this 1925-1926 Buick knocked the front door handle right off the car. The missing runningboard, twisted fenders and bumped rear bumper are among the car's other battle scars. Note the bald spare tire. "Handle" your old Buick with care — drive it carefully! (Frank Malatesta Collection)

An insurance photo, snapped on Feb. 2, 1937, reveals only minor damage to this 1925 or 1926 Buick sedan. The fender was bumped and the bumper was battered. This car had a book value of under $35 in 1937. Antique auto accidents can be expensive — drive your old car safely and save money! (Frank Malatesta Collection)

This Nash coach was around two-years-old when it had a fender-bender in Feb. 1927. The Nash next to it looks like a nearly new one. Damage is mainly in the area of the right rear fender. Drive your Nash safely! (Frank Malatesta Collection)

Though it would probably be restored today, the chances are good this 1929 accident put the four-year-old Chandler in a salvage yard. In addition to front fender and running-board damage, the hood, doors and rear quarter of the car's roof were banged-up in this crash. (Frank Malatesta Collection)

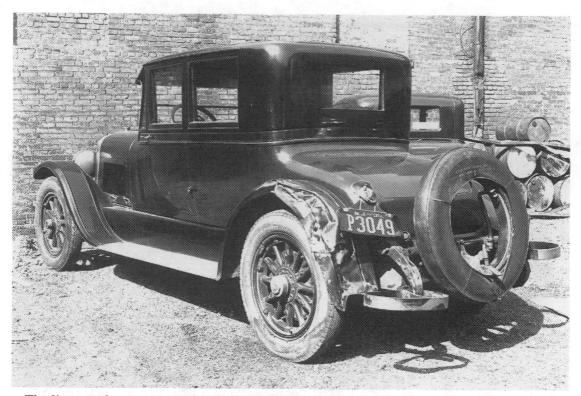

The license plate suggests that this Lincoln — a 1925 or 1926 model — was damaged in a 1935 accident. A used car guide of that year lists its worth as "salvage value." Leatherette spare tire cover promotes a Paterson, N.J. General Tire dealer. "Generally" speaking, safety is a must with antique autos! (Frank Malatesta Collection)

Photo taken on Sept. 5, 1933 shows only a small ding in the right rear fender of this 1926-1927 Model T Ford. However, the kinked front bumper, broken left rear quarter glass and missing steering wheel rim hint of extensive unseen damage. A careful look at the tires reveals a bent rim on the rear and an egg-shaped rim up front. Be a "good egg" — drive safely! (Frank Malatesta Collection)

Happily, slight damage to the rear fender appears to be the only thing wrong with this pretty 1926 Packard. Picture was taken on April 9, 1936. At the time, contemporary "blue books" listed this car's value as only around $200. (Frank Malatesta Collection)

Star cars were built in Elizabeth, N.J. from 1922-1928. This 1925 edition was wrecked in Paterson, N.J. in April 1929. Both front and rear fenders are dented. We wonder what happened to the roof? Look at the bald spare tire. Be a super "star" by driving safely! (Frank Malatesta Collection)

This sedan was hit by something big and heavy, or pushed into it. Notice how the spare tire left a tread print on the rear of the body. We couldn't pin down what type of car this is. Any guesses? (Frank Malatesta Collection)

In 1933, this car was worth only $60, so we doubt that this heavy accident damage was ever repaired. It's a 1926 Buick Master Six Model 48 four-passenger coupe. The use of worn out tires as a spare is seen again in this photo. "Master" highway safety before you hit the road in your Buick! (Frank Malatesta Collection)

Headlamp tie-bar was a new feature of 1926 Chevrolets. This sedan was pretty badly mashed in a June 1929 accident. Upper corner of the roof has fairly extensive structural damage. The owner of the car must have been a lover of window stickers. Drive safely in your vintage Chevrolet! (Frank Malatesta Collection)

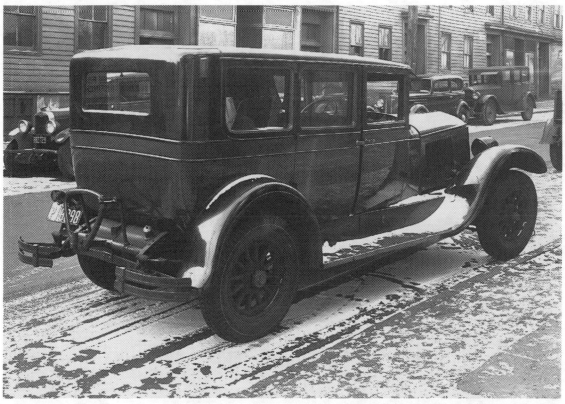

We guess this to be a 1927 Cadillac. Look at the angle of the hood after it suffered a front end impact. Right front fender and headlamps are out of kilter, too. The accident occurred in Dec. 1935. A 1927 Cadillac was worth just $281 then. (Frank Malatesta Collection)

Although this 1927 Model T Ford doesn't look too heavily damaged, notice the bulge in the roof and the broken rear quarter window. Apparently, the accident which bent the fenders was more than a fender-bender. The steering wheel rim is also missing. Drive your Model T carefully! (Frank Malatesta Collection)

Crinkled fender on 1928 Nash four-door sedan was easy to repair. It's hard to believe that the exterior finish on the rear fender is so deteriorated, as this car was only around two-years-old, when it was photographed on March 24, 1930. (Frank Malatesta Collection)

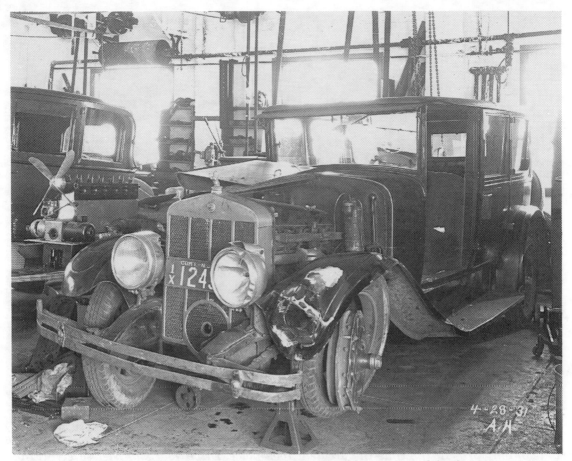

Commercial plates indicate that this 1927-1928 Franklin was used for business purposes, until it was damaged in an April 1931 accident. The collision knocked a tire right off its rim and took the driver's door off, too. (Frank Malatesta Collection)

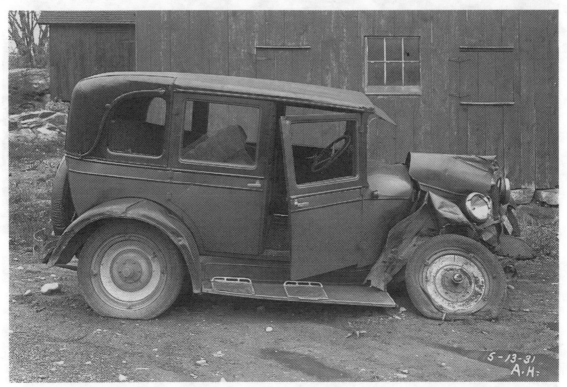

Pontiac name appears on the rear hubcaps of this wrecked sedan. It's a 1927 or 1928 model. Extensive front end damage, occurring during the May 1931 accident, certainly made this "Chief of the Sixes" a total loss. Drive your Pontiac carefully! (Frank Malatesta Collection)

Okay Chrysler fans — here's a beautiful car to restore. The 1928 convertible suffered only minor damage in this Nov. 1933 fender-bender and "bumper-dumper." This car had a book value of only $100 at the time the accident took place. Drive your Chrysler safely! (Frank Malatesta Collection)

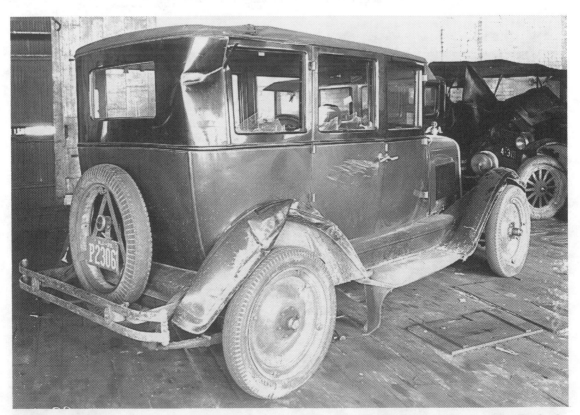

This 1925 Chevrolet sedan was damaged in a New Jersey accident in June 1929. Both the front and rear fenders were banged up, along with the rear door, quarter panel, running-board and roof. Glass in both rear side windows is shattered. Note the fancy hood ornament. The taillamp is not original equipment. See the U.S.A. (safely) in your Chevrolet! (Frank Malatesta Collection)

Here's a Pontiac that might make a good circle track car, as long as it traveled in the right direction! The 1929s were known as the "New Series," but this one was three years old when wrecked. Stay on the straight and narrow when you're driving an antique! (Frank Malatesta Collection)

Judging from the "H" viewable on the hubcaps with a magnifying glass, this is a Hupmo-bile sedan. It's probably a 1926 or 1927 model. The photo, taken on Nov. 28, 1930, shows rumpled fenders front and rear and broken glass. Keep your Hupp in top shape with careful driving! (Frank Malatesta Collection)

Bus number 90, used on the Paterson-Pompton Lake (N.J.) run in 1927, appears to have been built on a Pierce-Arrow chassis. It's probably an early 1920s model. On June 8 of that year this accident cut its run short. Drive your antique commercial vehicles safely! (Frank Malatesta Collection)

Parked in a lot near the National Ribbon Co. factory is a banged up 1927 Chrysler four-passenger coupe which was probably repaired. This model was new for 1927. The photo was taken on April 9, 1931. Note the vintage Esso gas pump and the Buick coupe in the background. Give your antique good gas and good driving! (Frank Malatesta Collection)

Dodge Brothers built this Standard Six four-door sedan in 1928. Four years later, it was involved in a smash up that wrecked its front and rear fenders and front hubcap. However, it would be considered an easy restoration project today. "Dodge" accidents before they happen — drive a safe-running car! (Frank Malatesta Collection)

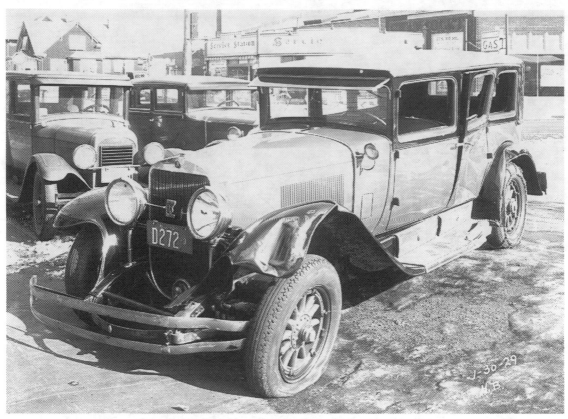

It looks like this 1928 Cadillac sedan was in nearly new condition when it was in a bad accident in Jan. 1929. There's snow on the roadway, which explains the chains on the rear fenders. The front fender looks easily repairable, but the damage to the rear quarter of the body is a bit more extensive. Note the "winterfront" on the Chrysler in the background. Go slow in the snow! (Frank Malatesta Collection)

Here's a 1928 Cadillac or LaSalle which was probably repaired after suffering a winter driving accident that crinkled its right rear fender. Note that the right rear bumper guard and spare tire are twisted out of shape, too. Drive carefully during the winter months! (Frank Malatesta Collection)

One man in this car
when it hit four other
car's on the highway near
selby laine.On Dec 24,1930.

One man was driving in this once-handsome-looking ragtop when it hit four other vehicles on a California highway near a street called Selby Lane. Despite extensive damage, no one was hurt in the Christmas Eve 1930 accident. Myles Hansen sent the photo, which was originally used in an **Old Cars Weekly** *editorial suggesting safe holiday driving in 1984.*

Big car — believed to be a 1929 Gardner sedan — has mainly sheet metal damage, which would certainly not prevent it from being restored nowadays. However, it was probably sold for salvage after this picture was taken. The photo is so clear that the words "Hood Rubber Company" can be seen on the sidewalls of the balloon tires. Check your vintage car tires carefully before setting off on a long tour! (Frank Malatesta Collection)

This 1928 Pontiac needs more than "graphite service" to get back on the road. In fact, it appears to be bound for the salvage yard. It would cost more to fix the car, than it was worth in Dec. 1931, when the accident took place. Note the nearly new, heavy-duty double white-wall tires. Pontiac lovers — send up a "smoke signal" for safe driving! (Frank Malatesta Collection)

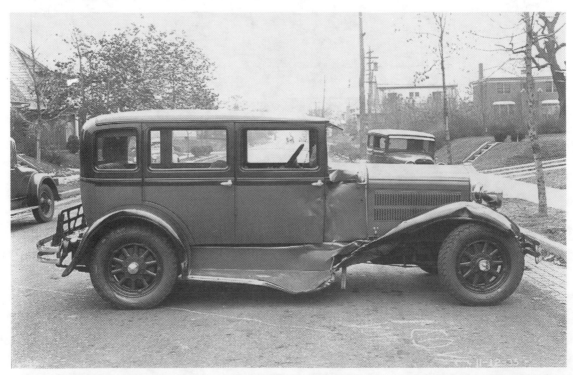

Nov. 12, 1935 accident twisted up this 1929 Hudson sedan in several places. Note the broken glass in the passenger side window. Also, notice the message "I love you" scrawled on the roadway. It proves that graffitti is nothing new. That appears to be a 1929 LaSalle parked behind the rear of the damaged Hudson. Keep your Hudson humming and drive it with care! (Frank Malatesta Collection)

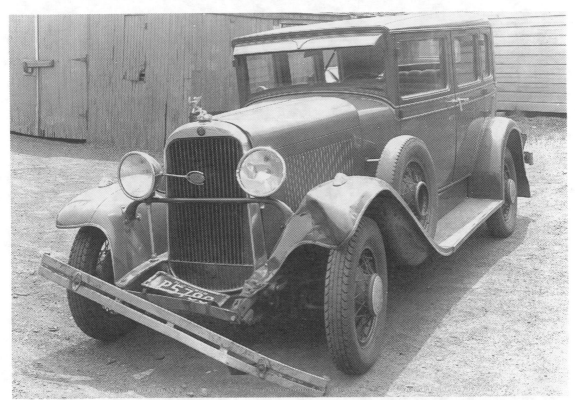

Peaked visor and flat double-bar bumper help identify this as a 1929 Oldsmobile F-29S deluxe sedan, of which only 7,197 copies were made. Deluxe equipment for this model included sidemounted wire wheels, trunk rack, front and rear bumpers and chrome plated headlamp shells. It sold for $1,105 when new, but was worth only a fraction of that when this accident occurred in June, 1932. Note the bald spare tire, the added-on fender lamps and the aftermarket hood ornament. Drive your Oldsmobile carefully! (Frank Malatesta Collection)

Fancy 1928 Studebaker Commander Six sedan suffered minor front end damage in this Oct. 1932 accident in New Jersey. The Commander was a new, mid-sized, mid-priced line for 1928. This Regal trim edition went for around $1,625. Dual sidemounts were an extra-cost option. Make safe driving "standard equipment" in your antique auto! (Frank Malatesta Collection)

Possibly the result of over-celebrating on New Year's Day, this wrecked Studebaker sedan was photographed on Jan. 10, 1936. It is a 1929 Commander Eight sedan, which sold for $1,375 when new. Note the rearview mirror mounted on a door hinge. Check all safety equipment, before leaving on a tour! (Frank Malatesta Collection)

Cars are speeding by in the background of this photo, but the 1929 Buick isn't going anywhere. Its left wheel, headlamp and fender are totally out of kilter. The bumper was displaced pretty badly, too. Driving on worn out tires seems to have been common during the depression. Keep safe tires on your vintage car! (Frank Malatesta Collection)

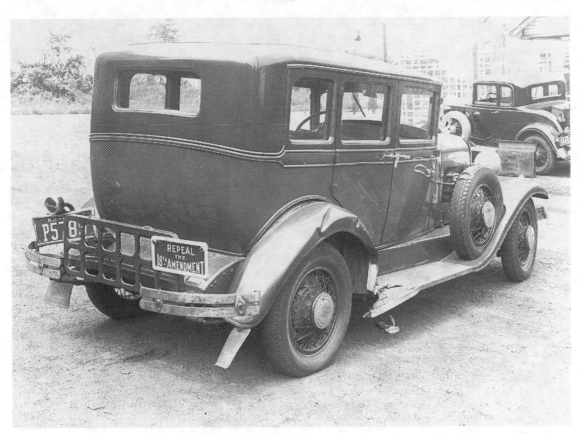

"Repeal the 18th Amendment" must have been on the mind of the owner of this 1929 Oldsmobile, reducing his driving alertness. The accident took place June 15, 1932. Damage included a smashed rear fender and torn runningboard. Several pieces of the front end look out of kilter. Drive your Olds carefully! (Frank Malatesta Collection)

Before it crashed in May 1934, this 1929 Nash had a "book value" of around $185. Notice the different style front and rear tires. How about that antique tractor parked behind the car? (Frank Malatesta Collection)

The Essex Super Six was known as a light, fast car. That may explain why we have come across photos of several wrecked examples. This one is a 1929 model. It was worth only around $130, in Sept. 1934, when this accident took place. (Frank Malatesta Collection)

Both 1929 and 1930 Hupmobiles look similar, but the lack of front fender parking lamps suggests that this is a 1929 model. It was clobbered pretty badly by another car, causing a great deal of damage to sheet metal and accessories. The bumper was torn right off the car. (Frank Malatesta Collection)

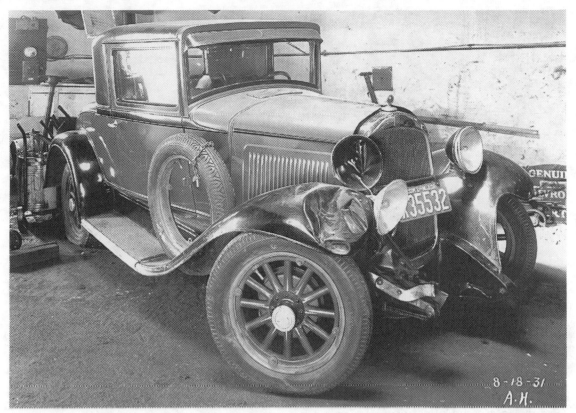

This car looks like it's trying to do the "Twist." We believe it's a 1929-1930 Whippet. This model was worth $625-$695 when new, but much less in this condition. Photo was taken April 18, 1931. Note the chain around the sidemounted spare tire. Drive your Whippet safely! (Frank Malatesta Collection)

An accident occurring in Jan. 1935 really banged-up this early 1930s Autocar truck. It appears to have flipped over, destroying the roof of the cab. Arrow Freight Lines — the truck's owner — operated in Paterson, N.J; New York, N.Y. and Scranton and Allentown, Pa. (Frank Malatesta Collection)

Here's a 1930 Essex Challenger Six that any Hudson fan would love to find and restore in 1990. A little body work and some new fenders would make this into a very nice car. The accident occurred on Nov. 21, 1933. Before being hit, the car had a "book value" of $147. (Frank Malatesta Collection)

The only damage to this 1930½ Dodge that shows in our photo is a dent on the top of its left front fender. When the picture was taken, by an insurance company photographer on Dec. 12, 1933, this beautiful MoPar had a "book value" of $133. How would you like to find one for that kind of price today? Drive your Dodge safely! (Frank Malatesta Collection)

This was a 1930 Packard, until it was mashed to pieces. The accident occurred on Oct. 4, 1935. The estimated value of this seven-passenger sedan, just before the crash, was a mere $135. Classics lost their value quickly during the Great Depression. (Frank Malatesta Collection)

The front wheel of this 1930 Essex was pushed backwards quite a bit by a wreck that tore up the right side of the car. Look at the cowl lamp dangling from its attaching bracket. Before this accident occurred, on Jan. 21, 1934, this standard coach had a "book value" of $188. Drive your Essex safely! (Frank Malatesta Collection)

This early 1930s Mack was operated by John Kimker Trucking, Inc. It had an accident that knocked the headlamp from the left fender. Note the "ICC" license plate and the battery sitting on the runningboard. The photo was taken on December 4, 1941. Keep on (antique) trucking, but do it carefully! (Frank Malatesta Collection)

A photo snapped on Nov. 21, 1933 shows how a 1930 Essex Super Six was knocked for a loop in a wintertime accident. The entire body of the car is "kinked" to the right. The bumper on that side of the car was pulled loose, but the bracket that once held it to the frame stayed put. (Frank Malatesta Collection)

Check out the front wheels on this rare beauty. They are both going in different direct-ions. Quite a bit of damage to runningboard, rear quarter of body and back fender is also apparent. Radiator badge reveals that the car is a Peerless. It looks like a 1929 Model 81 four-door sedan. Judging from photo, it snowed during mid-December of 1932 in New Jersey. Protect your Classic with "classy" driving habits! (Frank Malatesta Collection)

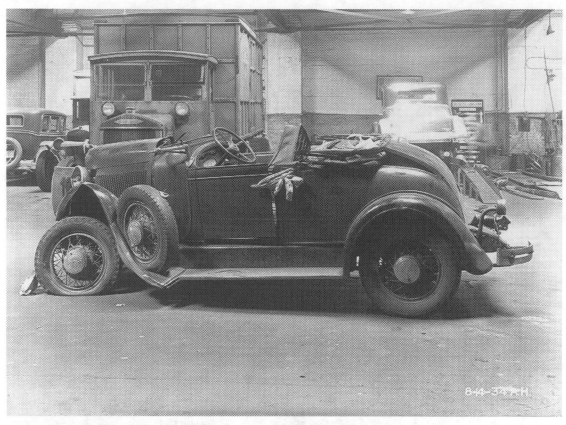

The door of this 1930 Oldsmobile had to be tied shut after the car was smashed in an accident on Aug. 14, 1934. Before the wreck, the value of the coupe-roadster was only $209! Notice the propeller hood ornament and the big Pierce-Arrow van type truck. Drive your Oldsmobile with care! (Frank Malatesta Collection)

This closed-bodied 1929 Essex Super Six nearly became a convertible sedan. From the looks of this Sept. 11, 1934 photo. It was hit very hard in the rear. At least the gasoline tank stayed intact, thanks to protection of heavy crossmember. Stay on top of all driving situations when you take your old car for a ride! (Frank Malatesta Collection)

Shop mechanics probably couldn't do very much for this severely damaged 1929 Essex Super Six, which appears to have rolled over in Sept. 1934. It has New Jersey license plates dated the same year. Drive your Hudson product safely! (Frank Malatesta Collection)

Both the fenders and the rear roof quarter of this 1929 Hupmobile sedan picked up sharp dents in a March, 1931 accident. The rear bumper and license plate are also twisted. Put a dent in the accident rate; practice safe hobby driving! (Frank Malatesta Collection)

It looks like someone "roped" themselves a badly battered 1930 Nash four-door sedan. Roll-overs like this one could tear apart the sturdiest-built automobiles. Notice the saddle on wall of garage in back of car. Horses had not been completely outmoded by May 25, 1934, when this picture was taken. Use horsesense when driving your old car! (Frank Malatesta Collection)

Believe it or not, the 1930 Oldsmobile convertible optioned with six wire wheel equipment was the most common example of this body style. Still, only 1,560 were built. This one survived four years, before it was wrecked in an Aug. 1934 accident. Be a survivor — drive your old car with extra care! (Frank Malatesta Collection)

Someone "restyled" the left front fender on this 1929 LaSalle and the parking light seems to be hanging on for dear life. A close look at photo, taken Dec. 17, 1932, also reveals broken glass sun visor. Safety tip: go slow in the snow! (Frank Malatesta Collection)

Classic Car Club of America members will be happy to see that this photo shows only minor damage to the front right-hand fender of the 1930 Packard. Difference in tire tread patterns suggests that a new tire may have been mounted after the crash. (Frank Malatesta Collection)

Here's a 1930 Oldsmobile convertible that lasted only two years before it was banged up in June 1932. Unlike many cars in the depression years, this one has good tires, including the spare. Maybe that's one reason the damage is relatively minor. (Frank Malatesta Collection)

Ill-fitting hood may be a sign of how sick the driver of this 1929-1930 Studebaker Eight felt after his or her accident. The right rear fender appears to be damaged in this photo taken on Sept. 19, 1933. As in many instances during the depression, the car owner was trying to get by with worn tires. Notice the covered wire wheel spare leaning against the wall and what looks like an automobile frame hanging from ceiling. (Frank Malatesta Collection)

"Dodge Brothers" name was last used on 1930 models, such as this handsome sedan which had a fender-bender accident on Dec. 12, 1933. "Dodging" your safe driving responsibilities is not a good practice! (Frank Malatesta Collection)

"No Smoking" is always a good idea around cars in an accident, since flammable liquids may be leaking. This doesn't seem true in the case of this 1930 Oldsmobile four-door sedan, which has mostly sheet metal damage. (Frank Malatesta Collection)

Mounting of cowl lamps at windshield post tells us this Essex sedan is a 1930 model. Side impact crash banged up just about everything from front fender to rear corner of roof. Broken wood spoke wheels were common in 1930s wrecks. (Frank Malatesta Collection)

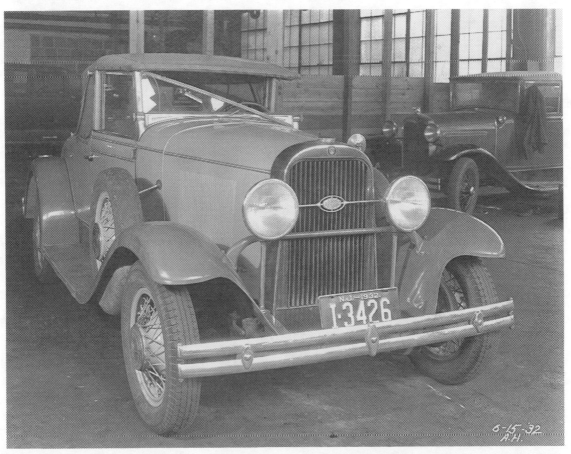

Rounded bumper bars date this accident-damaged Oldsmobile roadster to 1930. Only 2,970 of these cars were built. From this angle the windshield damage — most likely from an impact — is the only problem we can see. Deluxe equipment on this Olds included twin sidemounts, front and rear bumpers, a folding trunk rack and chrome headlamps. This package added $75 to the roadster's base factory price of $995. (Frank Malatesta Collection)

This 1930 Oldsmobile coupe-roadster has a trunk rack, but no trunk. Perhaps it bounced off when another car bounced into its rear fender and rear wheel rim. Take note of the side-mount support brackets and pedestal type rearview mirror attached to the left-hand spare. The accident occurred in June 1932. (Frank Malatesta Collection)

A dolly was required to get this 1931 LaSalle into a building used for storing wrecked cars. Photo — dated July 13, 1932 — shows LaSalle hubcap design, leatherette-covered side-mounts and pedestal mirror. Creases on fenders were a LaSalle feature. This car was only a year old, but it was probably written-off as a total loss. Drive your Classic carefully! (Frank Malatesta Collection)

This car lost part of its identity in a Jan. 1934 accident. The decorative bar between head-lamps was broken, hiding the fact that it's a 1930 Studebaker 8. Damage of this type was very typical of wrecks which occurred in this era. Keep your early '30s car from being damaged by driving it carefully! (Frank Malatesta Collection)

This photo could be titled "Silent Knight." The car is a 1930 Willys-Knight Model 87 four-door sedan and we're pretty sure it didn't make much noise after this accident! It came from a dealer with outlets in Butler and Pompton Lakes, N.J. (Frank Malatesta Collection)

Here's another case of front to rear sheet metal damage on a depression era car. In this case it's a 1931 Buick four-door sedan, which once carried a sidemounted spare. Bodies actually held up well in such accidents, but there was a lot of sheet metal to impact. (Frank Malatesta Collection)

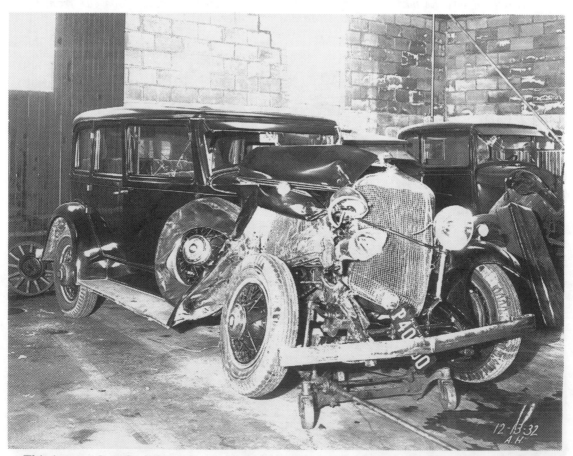

This is not what Cadillac ad copy writers had in mind when they mentioned the "penalty of leadership." Wrecked in the Dec. 1932 accident was a one-year-old Cadillac four-door sedan with sidemounts, which undoubtedly wound up in a salvage yard. (Frank Malatesta Collection)

Worn front tire may have contributed to this crash, which severly damaged a 1929 Chrysler series 75 convertible coupe. Originally priced at $2,995, production of this model was a mere 1,430 examples. Yet, the car was worth only around $125 when the accident occurred in April 1936. Note the steering gear parts dangling down. For a "good steer," point your antique car in a safe driving direction! (Frank Malatesta Collection)

When folks say they "get a lift" from old cars, this is not what they're talking about. We haven't been able to positively identify this model, which was hit in the rear in May 1931. Don't be "up in the air" about antique auto safety! (Frank Malatesta Collection)

This beautiful machine is a Peerless. Spotter's guide reference books lead us to believe it's a 1929-1930 four-door Brougham. Though priced in the $2,200 to $3,000 range when new, this model had a book value of just $150-$200 in 1931, when this wreck took place. (Frank Malatesta Collection)

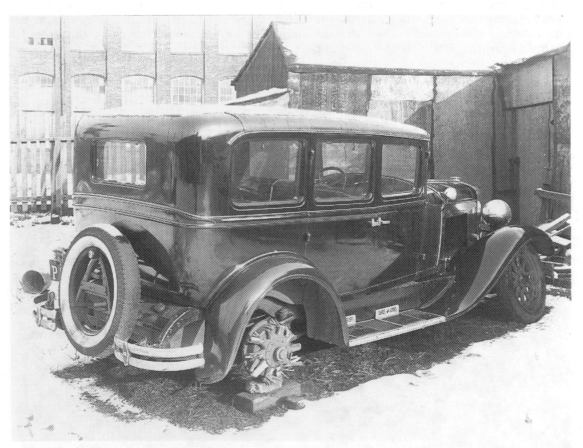

Split molding treatment at rear of body suggests that this beautiful car could be a 1929-1930 Peerless. Check out the remains of that wood-spoked artillery wheel. The spare tire is a whitewall and almost totally bald. Drive your Classic car safely! (Frank Malatesta Collection)

It's doubtful that this 1931 Packard coupe was fixed after this Dec. 1934 accident. Big cars lost value quickly during depression. Repair parts would have cost roughly $58.07 for welled fender, $76.50 for hood assembly, $25 for front bumper assembly, $75 for radiator shell and grille and around $37 (each) for all headlamp components. A new wire wheel, in prime, was $22.75. Compare these to modern prices and you'll realize it pays to drive antiques very carefully today. (Frank Malatesta Collection)

A crash that took place in Los Angeles turned this MoPar coupe on its roof. Writing on back of photo suggests the car is a 1932 Chrysler, but our research editor Ken Buttolph thinks it is a Dodge. The Los Angeles Police Department officer probably knows exactly what the car is. (Courtesy National Motor Museum, Great Britain)

It took a pretty hard hit to impact this 1929 Model A Ford's passenger door and running-board this badly. The back bumper didn't fare too well either. Accident occurred in early December, 1930, when car was two years old. Note the big roadster (a Chrysler) in the service bay. Help keep old car insurance rates low — drive carefully when you're touring! (Frank Malatesta Collection)

This photo, dated June 25, 1934, should inspire more than a few Model A Ford fans to travel a bit slower. The 1929 five-window coupe clearly lacked crash-proof bumpers. Right-hand tire is fairly nice, but the smashed one looks like a "baldie." (Frank Malatesta Collection)

A frontal impact was enough to knock the hood of this 1928-1929 Ford out of kilter. The right-hand end of bumper is pushed up against the bald tire. The Jan. 29, 1932 accident also cracked glass in the passenger door. Let's start "A" safety campaign — we can't "a-Ford" to wreck any more old cars! (Frank Malatesta Collection)

There were a lot of Fords on the road in December 1930. This one — a 1928 or 1929 sedan — seems to have had its days numbered. The body is so badly twisted that the hood no longer fits over the trusty four-banger engine. Drive your Ford safely! (Frank Malatesta Collection)

Linwall's Garage, a Dunlop Tire dealer, took in this 1928-1929 Model A Ford coupe after it was wrecked in June 1934. The car had a book value of around $124-$135 at the time of the collision. Note the gift box on the rear package shelf. Drive your Model A safely! (Frank Malatesta Collection)

This Ford hit something hard and solid. Notice how the fender has been pushed right over the flattened right front wheel rim. This accident occurred on July 16, 1934. Be careful when touring in your antique Ford! (Frank Malatesta Collection)

Black radiator finish suggests that this 1928-1929 Model A Ford is probably a roadster pickup truck. Even the radiator was twisted by the force of this fierce accident. "Blue book" value on this light commercial vehicle was about $68 when the wreck took place in Feb. 1933. Safe antique trucking is up to you! (Frank Malatesta Collection)

This Model A Ford Tudor sedan doesn't look heavily damaged, but we wonder why the door on the passenger side apparently doesn't close. Dented fender, broken glass and torn roof topping are other hints that it was in a wreck. Thanks to Bob Gassaway for the picture and for helping us drive home a hobby safety message.

The dual wipers have cleaned this Ford's windshield for the last time. Car can be identified as a 1930 Model A from design of radiator. The picture was taken July 20, 1931. Though only a year old, the tires are worn completely bald. Don't drive on "baldies." (Frank Malatesta Collection)

This photo has a definite "safety slant" to it. The Model A Fordor sedan looks like it was hit by something big. Damage to the rear right-hand side of the car is fairly extensive. Two old trucks parked behind the car do not appear to be wrecked. Drive your Model A safely! (Frank Malatesta Collection)

An Oct. 1933 accident made one of "Henry's Ladys" into a "lopsided Lizzy." Notice how the left-hand tire bead was broken by the crash. The bumper is twisted, the fender is crinkled and some suspension work seems to be in order, too. The car is a 1931 Model A roadster. (Frank Malatesta Collection)

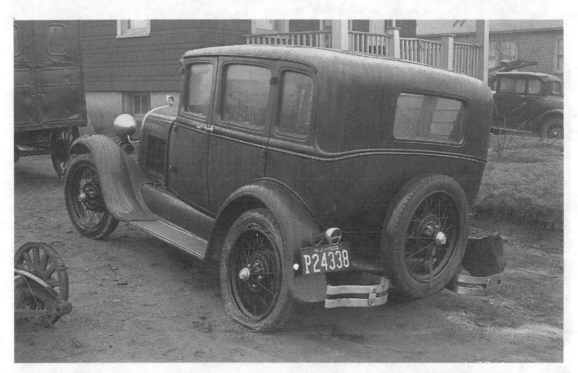

Large, thin wheels on depression-era cars were very susceptible to damage in motor vehicle accidents. This 1929 Model A's owner learned this lesson in Jan. 1932, when he wrecked his four-door sedan. Keep your wheels turning by driving safely. (Frank Malatesta Collection)

The 1939 California "World's Fair" license plates on this wrecked Model A Ford cabriolet must be collectible today. They actually promote the "Golden Gate Exposition," which took place on Treasure Island in San Francisco Bay. Exactly what caused the heavy damage isn't known. Photo is believed to be from the Myles Hansen collection and should inspire many hobbyists to "treasure" their antique cars by driving them safely on tours.

"My dad was a partner in the Ford garage in Rosalia, Wash., at the time this delivery truck overturned in 1930," advised Ray Brown, of Brown Auto Co. "His 1928 Model A wrecker was used to clear the wreckage." Ray notes that the first three vehicles were new 1930 Ford passenger cars and the fourth was a 1½-ton Model AA cab-and-chassis. We hope the photo delivers a safety message to many old car and antique truck hobbyists.

Here's a Model A Ford five-window coupe that took a bad beating on U.S. 40 near Jacksontown, Ohio, on June 13, 1952. It was hit in the rear by a cattle truck, which pushed it into a Trailways bus. The Ford's top was damaged as the car was scooped up on the front of the truck and laid into the rear of the bus. Jim D. Jones, of Cincinnati, works for Nationwide Insurance Co. and sent the photos. This reminds us that antique autos should always be properly insured.

An Ohio patrolman examines a Model A Ford that was damaged in a truck-car-bus entanglement. He must have had difficulty finding all the proper "10-codes" to write up the 1952 accident. The old wrecker in Jim D. Jones' photo would be nice to own today. Remember, though, that safe driving will help keep wreckers away from your antique autos!

An almost new Model A Ford roadster ran into this seven- or eight-year-old American LaFrance fire engine on June 29, 1930 in New Jersey. Judging from damage caused to the truck, this Ford was probably a total loss. Don't loose your antique Ford to careless driving! (Frank Malatesta Collection)

The owner of this 1929 Model A Ford Town Sedan probably found a good use for the sidemounted spare tire, since it looks like his right front wheel was ruined by this crash. Photo was taken on May 20, 1931. Remember that safety isn't a "spare" time responsibility; practice good driving all of the time! (Frank Malatesta Collection)

Hitchhikers may have been lucky that this 1930 Model A Ford truck permitted "no riders" to be picked up. Left front apron was twisted by whatever dimpled the left fender. Photo is dated July 5, 1933. Antique trucks need safe driving, too. (Frank Malatesta Collection)

Note the early Ford V-8 emblem on the spare tire cover promoting Toledo, Ohio's largest Ford dealer. The Model A was damaged in an accident that probably took place in 1932, judging by the license plate issue date. Photo came from Bob Gassaway, of Colts Neck, N.J., a well-known restorer and safe driving advocate.

Here's a 1930-1931 Model A Tudor sedan that would definitely be considered restorable today, despite minor accident damage to fenders, wheel and runningboard. Some mechanical problems seem to have also resulted from the crash. We hope that pictures such as this "transmit" a safe driving message. The photo was supplied by Wisconsin Power & Light Co.

Damage to this 1930-1931 Model A Ford sedan includes a rumpled right rear fender and a twisted bumper. The spare tire cover is very attractive and the car has a locking device to keep the spare tire from disappearing. This accident occured July 1931. (Frank Malatesta Collection)

Ford five-window Model A coupe didn't have a very long life. It was probably a dealer demonstration vehicle until it was heavily damaged in a Toledo, Ohio, accident which seems to have occurred in 1932. Restorer Bob Gassaway sent the photo. We hope that it inspired some hobbyists to drive their Fords safely in 1985, as we recommended when the picture first appeared in **Old Cars Weekly** that year.

Oops! The owner of this Ford, a 1930 Model A, bounced off something big and hard to damage the left fender that way. The balance of the car looks pretty good, but it probably has hidden impact damage. Note the fit of the hood and shattered windshield. Go slow when driving your Model A! (Frank Malatesta Collection)

Something had a "smashing" influence on the passenger side of this 1930-1931 Model A Ford Tudor sedan. The damage runs from the front of the car to the rear. Notice how bald the spare tire is. The other tires are probably just as bad. Safe tires are part of safe driving! (Frank Malatesta Collection)

Lopsided 1931 Model A Ford roadster had an accident which tore off edge of right front fender, kinked body panel alignment and re-arched headlamp tie-bar. Chrome windshield frame on left is missing. Note bald tires. Safe driver's ride on safe tires. (Frank Malatesta Collection)

This was a beautiful 1920s Packard, until a speeding train destroyed it on May 8, 1927. Towing dollies below the front and rear wheels were needed to move the remains of the vehicle to this service garage. The photo came from Myles Hansen to emphasize the need for safe operation of 1920s automobiles.

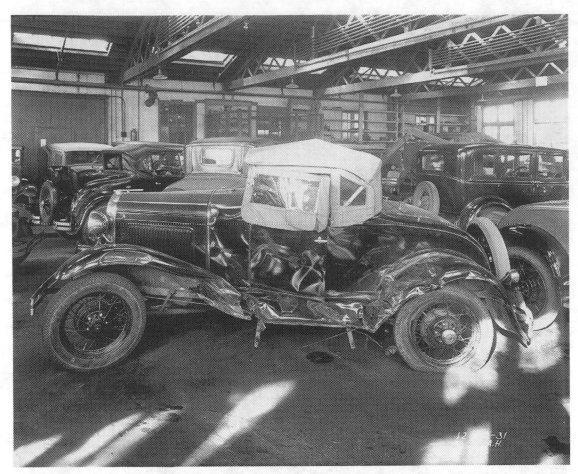

Side curtains can cut down your view of the road and may have been a factor in the crash that wrecked this 1930-1931 Model A Ford roadster in Dec. 1931. When driving with side curtains in place, always use extra care. (Frank Malatesta Collection)

Both sides of this 1930 Model A Ford Tudor were banged up in a July 20, 1931 accident. This is the least damaged side, probably the result of the car being pushed into something, after being struck by another vehicle at front left-hand corner. (Frank Malatesta Collection)

Using contrasting colors on moldings of Model A Ford roadsters was a popular dress-up trick. This 1930-1931 example, pictured after an Oct. 1934 accident, also has lights on front bumper, headlamp visors, front fender curb spotters and mud flaps on rear fender. If your Ford looks this good, drive it good, too. (Frank Malatesta Collection)

Occurring on Christmas Eve in 1933, the accident which damaged this 1930-1931 Ford resulted in some heavy fender-bending. Note how the owner of the car has refinished the body molding to give his Ford roadster a sportier than original appearance. Another photo in this book shows a second Model A roadster with similar customizing. Note that the hood ornament on this car is facing backwards! (Frank Malatesta Collection)

This 1940s Chevrolet wrecker appears to have been hit by a 1930-1931 Model A Ford while it was towing a 1937 LaSalle. Some good samaritans are on the scene to help with the clean up operations. (Photo courtesy National Motor Museum, Beaulieu, England)

Painted-in radiator shell tells us that this Model A Ford Sport Coupe is a 1931 edition. It appears to have been involved in a minor fender-bender during the wintertime. There's damage to the front and rear fender-sides, plus a missing hubcap. Notice the aftermarket accessory horn. Blow your horn for antique auto safety! (Frank Malatesta Collection)

A.E. Cron promised "reasonable, reliable, responsible" piano moving and hoisting, but the condition of his company's 1930-1931 Model AA Ford truck might make customers think twice about using the service "anywhere, anytime." Actually, the company from Jamaica, N.Y. was not responsible for this June, 1934 accident, which appears to have caused only slight damage to the moving van. Move safely in your old truck! (Frank Malatesta Collection)

Metalback 1931 Model A Ford Victoria sedan needs a new right rear fender, but not much else. The car must have been almost new when this accident took place in Oct. 1931. Accessory chrome "eyebrows" on headlamps add to its sporty looks. (Frank Malatesta Collection)

Oct. 28, 1931 insurance photo shows a new Model A Ford metalback Victoria sedan which suffered damage to front and rear fenders and roof. Note the curb spotters and headlamp visors — aftermarket add-ons seen on many Model As of the era. Remember, safe driving should be "standard equipment" for antique Fords! (Frank Malatesta Collection)

Painted-in radiator shell is a telltale sign of 1931 Model A Fords. Here we see a Tudor sedan that seems to have wound up in a junkyard, although accident damage is relatively minor. A car in this shape would surely be restored today, but not in May 1935, when photo was taken. Safe driving will keep your old car out of a junkyard! (Frank Malatesta Collection)

Someone remodeled the front end of this 1929 Buick with a immovable object. The car was probably scrapped because of this accident. The series 121 roadster was only two years old when this photo was taken on April 17, 1933. No doubt, today's restorers could find a way to use the rest of the body, which appears to be in excellent shape. Only 6,195 of these cars were built. Better-built Buicks demand better driving! (Frank Malatesta Collection)

Nov. 30, 1929, was the date of this unfortunate meeting between a Model T Ford touring and a 1928 Chrysler. Judging from photo, the older car got the worst of it, as the front end looks almost totally demolished. Accident took place in a New Jersey city. Safe driving is every old car hobbyist's responsibility! (Frank Malatesta Collection)

Bird's-eye view shows a 1928-1929 Essex Super Six which was hit in April 1929. Note how the door has been knocked out of alignment. The impact also caused loosening of the top covering material. How about those nifty parking lamp brackets? (Frank Malatesta Collection)

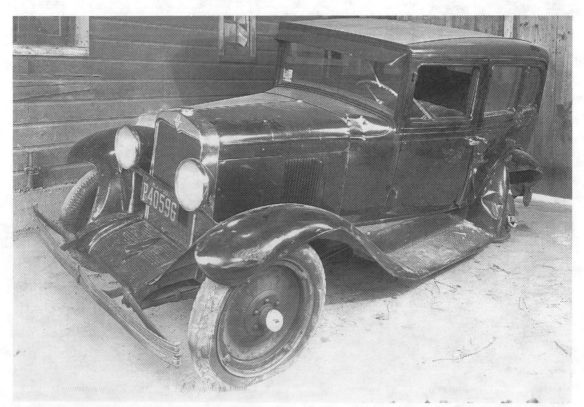

It looks like the driver of this 1929 Chevy four-door sedan was "grounded" after he had a wreck during 1933. It would be interesting to guess how the radiator and cowl became dented. Safe driving can keep your Chevy from becoming a three-wheeler! (Frank Malatesta Collection)

This 1929 Chevrolet looks like it received the "Coupe de grace" in a Jan. 22, 1931 photo. Something hit the Sports Coupe near the cowl and slid along the door, causing extensive sheet metal damage. Ice and snow were probably a contributing factor. (Frank Malatesta Collection)

Wet roadway may have caused this gravel truck to slide into the 1929 Chevrolet sedan. The car looks nearly new, but the April 17, 1930 wreck took away some of its shine. Hobby driving tip: slow up when it's slippery outside. (Frank Malatesta Collection)

And you thought the "Twist" was invented in the 1950s! This 1929 Chevy truck looks like it had the dance mastered way back in Nov. 1931. Depression-era truckers also had a hard time keeping new tires on their rigs. Good tires should be considered an important part of any antique truck restoration. (Frank Malatesta Collection)

The sight of a Model T Ford that was hit by a Southern Pacific train on Sept. 19, 1930 isn't a pretty picture. Although the quality of this old photo isn't the best, it's interesting to see the old-fashioned dollies beneath the rear tire and the antique gas pump. Good driver "training" is one way to help prevent car train wrecks. The photo came from Mylee Hanson.

When wrecked in March, 1931, this 1930 Chevrolet Universal AD Special Sedan was wearing a Model A Ford headlight on its right-hand side. The other side of the car has the stock Chevrolet type. Note the dented radiator shell (with unusual accessory hood ornament) and dented sun visor. Have a sunny day — drive safely! (Frank Malatesta Collection)

Today this Model T Ford roadster would probably be sold as a "rebuilder" for someone to fix up. The photo was exhibit no. 16 for a long ago court case in San Francisco. Lee Webber, of Santa Rosa, Calif. — the owner of a 1926 Model T — contributed the picture.

Cars with wood body framing didn't hold up very well in high-speed impacts, as indicated by this photo of a 1929 Chevrolet coach. Picture was taken after July 22, 1929 accident, as tow truck hauled the car into the shop. Don't blow your top on the highway; stay cool when you're touring! (Frank Malatesta Collection)

Odd-looking sun shades on headlamps give this 1929 Chevrolet coach a strange appearance. Something tore up the right-hand side sheet metal from front to rear and nearly ripped the passenger door off its hinges. (Frank Malatesta Collection)

This car would definitely be restored by a modern 1930 Chevrolet lover. It appears to have only minor right rear fender damage. Photo, snapped on Sept. 20, 1932, shows an accessory horn (near left-hand headlamp) and a door hinge-mounted outside rearview mirror. Rear tire below the dented fender is the only "baldie." This suggests that it was a spare tire, before the accident occurred. Spare nothing when it comes to safe hobby driving! (Frank Malatesta Collection)

This 1929 Chevrolet truck, owned by R. Weinman, has a 1933 New Jersey commercial license plate. It incurred severe damage to its radiator, headlamp, front and rear fenders and left-hand runningboard. A reflection in the windshield gives the illusion of that the truck has a stone roof pillar. Keep on truckin' and do it safely! (Frank Malatesta Collection)

Here's a car that definitely needs its headlights re-aimed. This photo of a wrecked 1930 Chevrolet sedan was taken March 6, 1931. The car appears to be heavily covered with road grime and rusty coolant sprayed from the damaged radiator. Check your antique car's headlamps for safer driving conditions! (Frank Malatesta Collection)

Chevrolet's third most popular model, the Independence AE two-passenger coupe, saw production of 51,741 units in 1931. This example was banged up in a June, 1933 accident. It seems to have brand new tires, but check out the condition of the spare. Keep your Chevy roadworthy. (Frank Malatesta Collection)

A dirty old truck pushed a sparkling clean 1929 Chevrolet up on the sidewalk, during this accident. It occurred on April 17, 1930, at Fourth Avenue and Utter Avenue, in Paterson, N.J. (Frank Malatesta Collection)

Unlike "Today's Chevrolet," yesteryear's did not have a five-mile per hour bumper! The double-bar type on this 1930 four-door was twisted as badly as other front end parts. Accident occurred in March, 1931, when car was near new. Whether it's yesterday, today or tomorrow, driving your vintage Chevy with care is a good idea! (Frank Malatesta Collection)

Bald tires must have contributed to many accidents in the 1930s, including the wreck of this 1929 Chevrolet sedan. When this car was banged-up on Nov. 21, 1933, it had a "book value" of just $113. Note the factory type, center-mount taillamp, which is hard to find at antique auto swap meets today. (Frank Malatesta Collection)

"It looks like a water tower or windmill fell onto this car," wrote Paul Lebitsch, Jr., the Clifton, N.J. old car hobbyist who found the old picture postcard. This may be a case where safe parking was more important than safe driving.

With their wood body framing, cars of the early 1930s would often suffer massive structural damage in collisions. This 1931 Chevrolet coach is a good example. There doesn't seem to be one straight body panel left on the nearly new "Stovebolt." In fact, it would not even make a good parts car for a restoration. The photo, supplied by Wisconsin Power & Light Co., reminds us that we must all play our "parts" in the safe driving of restored old cars.

Sidemounted spare on this 1931 Chevrolet Independence series four-door sedan was knocked right off the wire wheel rim by force of front end collision. It appears that the car is nearly new and the condition of the tires would back up his view. Don't practice your "Independence" on the highway; follow all safety rules! (Frank Malatesta Collection)

Well-equipped 1931 Chevrolet Independence AE four-door Special Sedan was hit pretty hard in the front, damaging fender aprons and frame and knocking off its bumper. The crankhole cover is missing and everything up front seems to be kinked a bit. Note the many accessories, such as a deluxe hood mascot, dual wire wheel sidemounts with metal covers and chrome trim and pedestal mirror on left-hand side. Photo dates from Sept. 10, 1934. Drive your antique Chevy safely! (Frank Malatesta Collection)

Stan Shirley, of Memphis, Tenn., sent this fender-bender photo. He noted, "This accident is believed to have been caused by Baron Van Harvey, of Harvey Carriage Works. Reports said he was looking at a girl who was standing in the snow wearing only a bathing suit." When you drive your old car, don't let distractions slow your reactions!

Viewing this photo might be described as checking the "tow-in" on a 1930 Chevy. The sidemounted four-door sedan has a lot of damage to front sheet metal (note left headlamp and cowl lamp), as well as scratches and dents above rear door. Touring trunk and rack on rear were extras. Remember, it's a "Universal" fact that safe driving pays! (Frank Malatesta Collection photo)

This 1930 Chevrolet Universal AD Special Sedan came standard with six wire wheels, front and rear bumpers, plus a dome lamp, robe rail and silk assist straps. The steamer trunk and rack mounted on the rear were extras. Chevy built 35,929 copies of this model. This car, owned by a family from Astoria, N.Y., was not very old when it was damaged in a 1931 crash in New Jersey. (Frank Malatesta Collection)

On May 21, 1932, this new Chevrolet coupe with only 600 miles on the odometer was hit by a large truck at the intersection of two streets — Main and Bayshore — in an unidentified California city. Note the sidemounted spare tire with chrome trim ring, fancy hood mascot and old-fashioned tow dollie. Myles Hansen contributed the photo as another reason to drive safely.

Photo snapped in Oct. 1933 shows a sideswiped Studebaker which was probably fixed to look as good as new. Notice how bald the rear-mounted spare tire is. In 1933 it cost about $26 for a Studebaker front fender and around $15.50 for a rear one. A runningboard assembly sold for $7.50. The car is a 1927 model. Keep your "Studie" steady, drive with care. (Frank Malatesta Collection)

We're quite sure this 1932 Chevrolet was never fixed. The rear of the car looks like it was torn apart by the accident. Even a good Confederate Sport Roadster could be purchased for just $280 when this photo was taken in Aug. 1934. Drive your Chevy to the levy safely! (Frank Malatesta Collection)

An old photographers' magazine ran this photo of a smashed-up 1929 Auburn phaeton with an article about selling pictures of auto accidents. Prints of this accident were sold to five newspapers for $5 each.

This is a side view of an almost-new 1932 Chevrolet Deluxe coupe that was clobbered by a large truck on May 21 of that year. This Chevy must have been a dandy before it was wrecked, with its full load of shiny factory accessories. Myles Hansen sent the picture, which inspires us to warn that safety should not be considered an "accessory" to antique auto operation.

This big Studebaker — probably a 1930 model — met an immovable object on July 16, 1934 on a New Jersey highway. The car has one black sidewall tire and one whitewall. The covered sidemounts and touring trunk were extra-cost accessories. Steer your Studebaker down the road to oafc driving! (Frank Malatesta Collection)

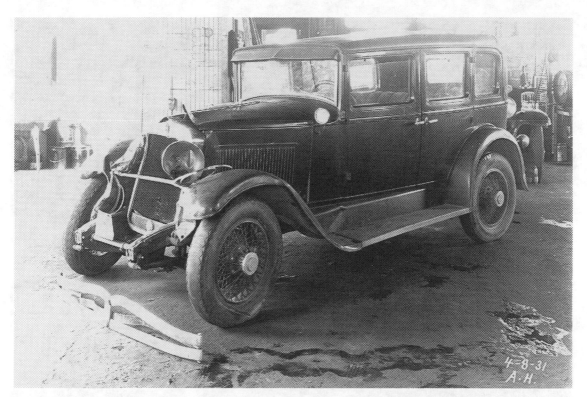

Hupmobile sedan was "restyled" by a frontal impact on April 8, 1931. It's a 1929 model and must have some mileage on the "clock," if the condition of the tires is any indication. This model cost $1,395 when it was brand new. Preserve automotive history with careful driving habits! (Frank Malatesta Collection)

Buick owners will be happy to see only minor damage to the front right fender of this 1930 two-door sedan, which has chrome-trimmed, metal-covered, wire wheel sidemounts and whitewall tires. Photo was taken July 21, 1933 in the city of Paterson, N.J. When better cars are built, it pays to drive them better! (Frank Malatesta Collection)

Accident damage to this 1931 Hudson was documented by insurance company photographer on Aug. 25, 1932. Some replacement parts costs at time were: $14.50 for front fender, $36.75 for hood assembly, $7.35 for runningboard assembly, $15 for headlamp assembly and $9 for rear fender in prime. Parts cost a lot more today, so drive your Hudson with care. (Frank Malatesta Collection)

This 1932 Chevy is heavily loaded with both accessories and body damage. The Series BA roadster sold for $445 in standard trim, but the sidemounts (knocked off in the accident), bumpers, hood mascot, trunk rack and chrome louver doors were extras. Cars in back are (left-to-right) a Hudson, a 1931 Buick, an unidentified model, a 1933 Pontiac and a 1933 Plymouth. (Frank Malatesta Collection)

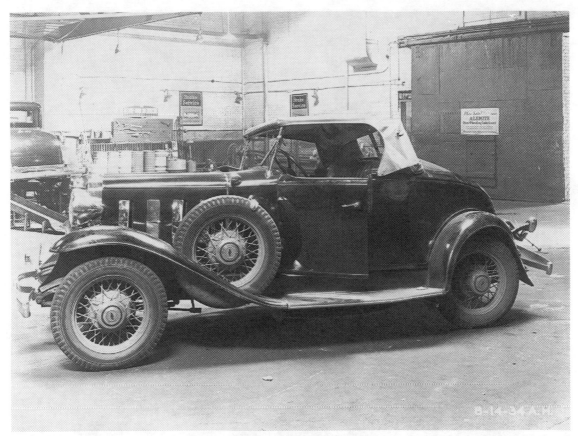

Here's another car that makes old car hobbyists vividly aware of the importance of safe driving. Just 8,552 of these 1932 Chevrolet Confederate BA Deluxe Sports Roadsters were built. This Aug. 14, 1934 photo says a lot about why we're promoting the theme of driving hobby vehicles extra-carefully. (Frank Malatesta Collection)

Nearly new 1933 Chevy Sport Coupe was wrecked in July of that year. This model sold for $535. It might be a little hard to climb into that rumbleseat, judging from the way the sheet metal surrounding the lid has been damaged. (Frank Malatesta Collection)

April 28, 1933 photo shows front view of almost new 1933 Chevy Master sedan which, apparently, has damage to both sides of its body. We'd guess that impact occurred on passenger side, since wheel rim there was destroyed. Keep a sharp eye peeled on both sides of the road when driving old cars! (Frank Malatesta Collection)

This accident took place in 1916 near Pierson, Iowa. The car is a near-new Reo touring. Notice the white rubber tires. Wood spoke wheel was shattered by the impact. Keep your antique "wheels" turning safely! (Dale V. Nafe photo)

Another example of a car — a 1933 Chevrolet Master four-door sedan — showing what is probably the most common type of accident damage from this era. Some repair parts costs for this model are: $11.45 for front fender, $6.75 for rear fender, $9.45 for runningboard assembly, mat and brackets, $4 for rear quarter glass, plus $17.50 for body labor to repair doors. This car was near-new when photo was snapped on April 28, 1933. (Frank Malatesta Collection)

This 1933 Chevrolet seems to have faired pretty well, considering it was hit by a commuter bus. The larger vehicle has a 1949 Wisconsin license plate. Believe it or not, the Chevy had a cash value of just $95 when it was wrecked, while its retail value in 1949 was a mere $145. The photo was provided by Jeff Gillis of the Durant Family Registry, a hobby organization headquartered in Green Bay, Wis.

That's not a rifle club sticker on the windshield of the 1933 Chevrolet Master Eagle CA Sports Roadster. Back then, NRA meant National Recovery Act and consumers used such stickers to show that they were making efforts to curtail the depression. At a glance, damage to this car isn't obvious, but take a close look at the fit of the hood, shape of the grille, distorted right-hand horn and bent license plate. Just 2,876 copies of this $485 model were made. Photo was snapped Oct. 23, 1933, so the car was nearly new. Don't cause depression — drive your valuable antique car safely! (Frank Malatesta Collection)

This 1933-1934 Chevrolet coach was extensively damaged in an accident which occurred in March or April of 1934. In addition to the body sheet metal being mashed, the top covering on the roof was affected by the crash. Keep on top of hobby safety by driving your Chevy carefully! (Frank Malatesta Collection)

The hood ornament of this 1934 Chevrolet coach was knocked completely sideways by a frontal collision. The photo was snapped on March 19, 1935. The average cash value of this model, in good shape, was $320 at that time. (Frank Malatesta Collection)

Undated photo shows a 1933 Chevrolet Master Eagle sedan that took a wallop from a big car or truck. License plates from New Jersey are 1933 issue, suggesting that this was a new automobile when it was wrecked. The sedan sold for $565 and 162,361 copies were made, so at least this isn't a rare model. Mote the Model A Ford in the background. (Frank Malatesta Collection)

The Cord L-29 two-/four-passenger cabriolet sold for $3,295 when it was introduced. By 1932, the price had to be cut $800 to encourage sales of this model during the depression. This example (model year undetermined) has all the "goodies," such as sidemount spare tires, a spotlamp, double whitewalls. It also has some front end damage. Only one of the spares is covered and none of the tires on the car are in very good shape. Careful cruising in your Cord! (Frank Malatesta Collection)

This coupe plowed into the porch of a house and it looks as if the house had more clout. The make of the car isn't known, but its body styling looks much like that of a Chevrolet or Pontiac model. Notice how the rear of the hood went right through the windshield. (Frank Malatesta Collection)

Large series 1930 Buick was towed into a repair shop on March 10, 1933, following a sub-stantially damaging collision. The car's rear fender was peeled away from the body. Maybe the flat tire on the rear could not be replaced because the sidemounted spare tire had disappeared. The Buick was worth $75-$100 at the time of the accident. (Frank Malatesta Collection)

Only minor fender work would be required to make this 1930 Packard look like new again. The front fender appears to be in the worst shape. Damage appraisal photo was snapped on April 15, 1936. Drive your Packard safely! (Frank Malatesta Collection)

This 1930-1931 Studebaker was badly mangled in a side impact collision. The estimated value of this beautiful car, at the time of this crash on Sept. 19, 1933, was in the range of $470. Drive your Studebaker safely! (Frank Malatesta Collection)

It's likely that this 1932 Essex-Terraplane coupe rolled over. Damage is apparent at three spots on the roof, plus all of the running gear and rear quarter area. Originally priced at $510, the coupe had only salvage value after this Jan. 1934 accident. Keep your Hudson on a safe course! (Frank Malatesta Collection)

Want to bet this 1932 DeSoto convertible isn't in the shop for a brake fluid check? It may need some of the advertised services, however, before the accident damage is repaired. Photo was taken Aug. 16, 1932, when the car was nearly new. The Custom SD six-cylinder DeSoto model originally cost $750 and only 2,705 standard and Custom versions were ever built. Explore safe driving in your DeSoto! (Frank Malatesta Collection)

The doors of this dented Pierce-Arrow Victoria Coupe had to be tied together following an accident which caused damage to the passenger side. This car retailed for $3,475, but had a "blue book" value of only $710, in Sept. 1934, when it was smashed-up. Drive your Pierce as straight as an arrow! (Frank Malatesta Collection)

Chrysler made its last roadster in 1932. Judging from the rearward location of the door handles, this appears to be one of the final batch. The accident damage is basically limited to the sidemount spare tire cover, fender apron, runningboard and door. This car was probably fixed. Drive your Chrysler safely! (Frank Malatesta Collection)

Rare 1930½ Chrysler convertible coupe looks repairable. We're sure that every old car hobbyist hopes that it was fixed-up and preserved for a future collector. Accident damage is basically restricted to front fender, door skin and runningboard. Drive your Chrysler safely! (Frank Malatesta Collection)

We're sure that a Dodge collector would restore this one quickly. It's a 1933 model that suffered a crash on Oct. 1, 1935. This car's "blue book" value at the time of the accident was just $265. Note how the front end was crinkled by the impact. Drive your Dodge carefully! (Frank Malatesta Collection)

Luckily, this pretty 1931 Chrysler Deluxe Eight five-passenger coupe — one of 1,506 made — has only minor damage to right rear fender. A brand new fender for the $1,535 automobile was only $15. The coupe is a Royal Special, with goodies like twin horns and sidemounts. Drive your vintage Chrysler carefully! (Frank Malatesta Collection)

This accident turned the right-hand headlamp into an aircraft searchlight! The 1932 Essex was mashed by a head-on collision occurring in Jan. 1934. We would guess that one of the tires had to be changed to move the vehicle to the repair shop, but did they mount the bald spare or put a new tire on the right-hand front rim? Good tires and good driving seem to go together! (Frank Malatesta Collection)

A car-train wreck is one of the most deadly types of accidents. This one occurred at 7:45 a.m. on Aug. 30, 1930 when a Southern Pacific train hit an early Dodge touring car. Myles Hanson sent the photo, which underlines the need to exercise extreme care, at railroad crossings, when touring in restored antique autos.

Woman peering from window of house doesn't look too happy about the condition of this 1933 Plymouth, which was wrecked in a 1936 accident. Heavy snow and bald tires were probably contributing factors to car's demise. (Frank Malatesta Collection)

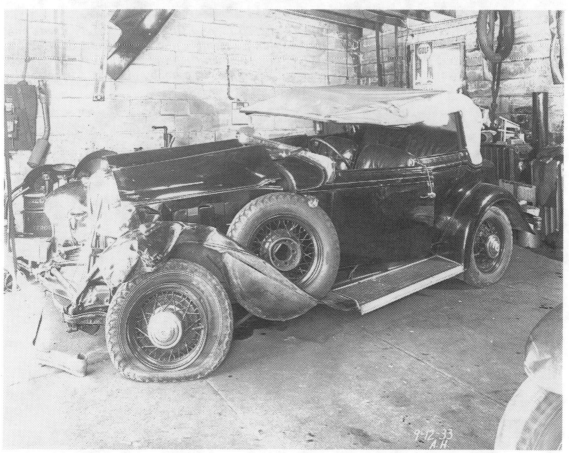

This 1932 buick is a rare two-door, five-passenger Convertible Phaeton. This body style was introduced in all series that year. We believe this is the 90 series version, of which only 269 were built, including one exported car. Photo dates from Sept. 12, 1933 and it's doubtful the car was repaired. (Frank Malatesta Collection)

A new welled fender for this 1933 Dodge cost $26.35, and this car definitely needs one. Add $27.50 for a radiator shell, $13.75 for headlamp assembly and $8 for front bumper bar and you can see that the car — worth about $275 when wrecked in Oct. 1935 — most likely went to a salvage yard. Don't "dodge" your responsibility as a hobby motorist; drive safely! (Frank Malatesta Collection)

The body seems to have been flung from the chassis of this car, which was in a collision that occurred during August 1917 in Poughkeepsie, N.Y. Gary R. Schmidt, of Youngstown, Ariz. found the old picture postcard showing the wreck. Keep your old car's body intact by practicing safe driving habits.

Here is a second 1933 Plymouth which was totaled in a bad wreck. The accident damage photo is dated Sept. 12, 1933, so the car must have been nearly new. However, fixing it seems to be out of the question. Drive your old Plymouth safely! (Frank Malatesta Collection)

An early example of a "parts car" is this 1934 Plymouth four-door sedan, wrecked in Feb. 1942. The wheels and tires were quickly removed for use on another car and the interior is completely gutted. Still, many good body and trim components remain on the hulk. Don't let your old car become a parts car; do your part for safe hobby driving! (Frank Malatesta Collection)

It looks like this little 1933 Plymouth really got banged-up in this accident. The frame below the cowl is badly bent and the radiator is completely missing. Notice the gasoline tank peeking out from below the rear fender. Drive your Plymouth carefully! (Frank Malatesta Collection)

Tarp on roof was probably used to protect the engine of this 1933 Plymouth PC sedan, after a Feb. 1936 accident took the front end sheet metal almost totally away. This model was Plymouth's first six, selling for $575 when it was new. The company made 33,815 of them for the U.S. market. Note the running board step plates. These are rarely seen today. (Frank Malatesta Collection)

Early Ford V-8 Club members will be interested in this photo taken on July 30, 1936. It shows a two-year-old Model 40 Fordor sedan which took a hard clout in the right rear quarter region of its body. Notice how bald the tires are. Ford built 22,394 of these in standard trim, but produced 102,268 as Deluxe equipped models, which had pinstriping, cowl lights, twin horns and two taillamps. This car has Deluxe equipment. (Frank Malatesta Collection)

All 1934 Pontiacs had straight eight engines. The cabriolet sold for $765. It survived only one year, before being badly wrecked in April 1935. It's a standard equipped version, as indicated by the Indian head within a circle hood ornament. Bumper, radiator and left front fender took a really hard impact. Drive your Pontiac safely! (Frank Malatesta Collection)

An Aug. 1937 accident rumpled the hood and fenders of this 1934 Ford cabriolet, not to mention the broken glass and twisted headlamps and cowl lights. The 40 Series "Early V-8" convertible sold for $590, including the rumbleseat. Ford made 14,496 of these. Drive your Early V-8 Ford safely! (Frank Malatesta Collection)

This 1933 Oldsmobile eight was involved in a front fender-bender. The touring sedan model sold for $995 when it was new. Oldsmobile made 1,345 examples with sidemounted spare tires. This photo is from July 2, 1931. Drive your antique Oldsmobile safely! (Frank Malatesta Collection)

The only damage we can see in this Jan. 8, 1936 photo is a shallow dent on the 1935 Buick's metal sidemount tire cover. Something must have dropped or fallen on it. Oh well, an insurance photographer's life isn't always exciting! Keep your Buick out of the way of falling objects! (Frank Malatesta Collection)

From the cowl back, this 1934 Chrysler Airflow Custom Eight has hardly any damage, except for a missing runningboard. The car seems to have all the "goodies," including fender skirts. We wonder if that's its grille lying on the shelf behind? Safe driving in your streamliners! (Frank Malatesta Collection)

This car probably had better "airflow" to the engine, after its Aug. 1935 accident. Actually, it's a 1934 Chrysler Airflow Custom Eight four-door sedan. The streamliners were introduced in 1934, but failed to gain popularity with new car buyers. Note the unusual pattern of the General Tires, which were factory equipment on this car. Keep a safe "air" flowing when you drive your vintage Chrysler! (Frank Malatesta Collection)

Whatever hit this 1935 Ford inflicted heavy sheet metal damage to the right-hand side of the vehicle. The windows and windshield didn't fare very well either. Wire spoke wheels were standard on Fords for the last time in 1935. Bob Gassaway provided the photo as a safe driving reminder to follow hobbyists.

We would guess that this 1935 Ford five-window coupe was a "fixer." Cost of a new, painted rear fender was just $9 at the time. Runningboard assembly sold for $5.32, plus $1.15 for two moldings. New hubcaps were only 85¢ each! That adds up to $16.32 for complete job. Fords cost a lot more to fix today, so drive them a lot more safely. (Frank Malatesta Collection)

A tow truck hauls away a 1935 DeSoto sedan which slid off a snowy Illinois roadway. Notice the aftermarket spotlamp. Photo taken by accident and safety photographer James W. Seymour is from the Randy Fleischhauer Collection.

Snow causes many accidents. This one took place on East Washington St., in Madison, Wis., on Valentine's Day 1949. How sad that this 1935 Dodge made it through the war years in such fine shape, only to wind up this way. A contemporary used car price guide shows that its cash value at the time of the wreck was only $110-120. Its base value (less repairs) was in the $125-135 range and it had a suggested retail value of just $165-180. The photo was taken by Elmer Nordness of the Madison Water Uitlity and sent in by Jim Kelly.

This unidentified brass era touring car wound up in a repair shop following a wreck which heavily damaged the front end. Right-hand steering was common prior to 1913. Steer clear of accidents; practice safety on the highway! (Courtesy Jaguar Cars of North America)

A Pennsylvania Railroad train hit this 1935 Ford on a country road near Brookville, Ohio, on Feb. 28, 1954. The amount of damage seems relatively light for this particular type of wreck. Jim D. Jones, of Cincinnati, provided the picture and information. When driving on antique car tours, always be extra cautious when approaching unguarded rail crossings.

Badly damaged front fender made a mess of this pretty 1935 Dodge New Value Line Six when it was 14-years-old. Since damage is confined mainly to replaceable parts, such as fender, wheel, bumper, grille and headlamp bucket, the car may have been fixed. The approximate cost of parts at the time of the wreck would have been $26.50 for the fender; $11.55 for the wheel; $14.40 for a front bumper (plus $3.15 for guards); $69.85 for a new grille and $16.50 for the headlamp. While the front license plate carries a 1947 expiration date, Elmer Nordness of the Madison Water Utility snapped this photo Feb. 14, 1949. Jim Kelly sent it to **Old Cars Weekly**.

This truck owned by the Madison Wis., Water Utility was involved in a collision near the State Fairgrounds on Dec. 5, 1938. We think that it might have been a rare 1935 Plymouth pickup. Jim Kelly sent in the Elmer Nordness" photo. The scene sparks a suggestion to drive extra carefully when the roads are wet or icy.

A car failed to halt for a stop sign. It hit the side of this 1937 Dodge sedan, doing major damage and sending the car flying into a pole which had two stop signs mounted on it. "Three people were injured," notes a Baraboo, Wis. car buff who signs his name as "Mr. Ed." He sent the picture to us and we hope it leads many old car hobbyists to take extra care at stop signs.

While traveling between Kansas City and Hannibal, Mo., in April 1949, Charles L. Jensen came upon this accident. The Joliet, Ill. old car buff advises that this 1936 Chevrolet blew a tire and rolled over. Four or five people riding inside were injured and taken to a hospital. You can see the 1948 Plymouth that Mr. Jensen drove at the time in the background at left.

No details accompanied this photo of what appears to be a 1936 Chevrolet sedan, which was totally wrecked in a bad collision. The twisted remains of the vehicle make a strong statement about the need for safe operation of collector cars on the highways. Myles Hansen sent this picture.

When this 1937 DeSoto hit a garage in Sayreville, Long Island, N.Y. in March 1946, the structure collapsed on the vehicle. This knocked one headlamp completely off the fender, as shown in photo by Jim Fitchett. The auto had a cash value of $375. We urge you to keep your old car in a safe garage, so it doesn't wind up under it!

You have to wonder how this 1937 Plymouth sedan sustained so much damage to its radiator without the bumper being bent. Most likely, it was hit amidships, on the right-hand side, and slid into something that the bumper slid over. When you slide into the seat of your antique Plymouth, keep safe driving in mind! (Frank Malatesta Collection)

Olds lovers will be happy to see that this 1936 model has hardly any significant accident damage. The right-hand headlamps is slightly out of kilter and there appears to be a shallow dent in side panel just below it. Photo is dated June 1, 1936. Keep your Olds "mobile" by practicing good highway habits. (Frank Malatesta Collection)

The driver of this old pickup was arrested for reckless driving after causing a wreck that seriously injured three people. He attempted to pass the sedan seen here and hit an oncoming vehicle head-on. The accident occurred in Fond Du Lac County, Wis., according to "Mr. Ed.," of Baraboo.

Here's an example of an extremely rare Chrysler that suffered a tragic fate. The Model C-8 Airstream convertible sedan was one of just 362 built in 1936. This car also had some hard-to-find extras such as covered sidemount spares, factory fender skirts and a radio. Most hobbyists will agree that owners of particularly rare cars surviving today should be extra careful when driving. After all, the preservation of automotive history is important to everyone involved in the hobby and tragedies like this one are detrimental to our cause.

This new 1936 LaSalle must have been tapped in the rear by another car which slid in the snow. You can see that the left end of the rear bumper looks too close to the body, while the right end is pushed out too far. Remember putting tire chains on in the winter? Drive your LaSalle safely! (Frank Malatesta Collection)

A damaged 1937 Plymouth coach illustrates a few aftermarket accessories that were used to personalize its appearance. They include "Buick portholes" bolted to the hood and non-MoPar front bumper ends. The truck in the background is an International. Safety is an international concern of old car hobbyists — drive safely wherever you go! (Frank Malatesta Collection)

*According to **The Standard Catalog of Light-Duty American Trucks**, this styling was introduced on Divco delivery trucks in 1937. But, the new look did not include dented bumper and front sheet metal, caused by an accident. Curb side of Borden's dairy truck also has damage to body, door and rear fender. (Frank Malatesta Collection)*

You didn't know that Dodge made compact cars in 1938? Of course, this isn't so. This full-sized sedan was turned into a compact by an accident that occurred on June 9, 1950. The collision took place on U.S. Highway 40 east of Hebron, Ohio. Jim D. Jones, of Cincinnati, sent the picture as a safe driving reminder. Safety should not be a "small" consideration with hobbyists!

A front end collision put this 1938 Pontiac two-door slantback out of commission. The 1948 New Jersey license plate suggests that the car was 10-years-old at the time it was wrecked. It's a Pontiac six, with plain hood louver styling. Note the chrome wheel trim rings. Pontiac fans make auto safety a "chief" concern! (Frank Malatesta Collection)

Damaged 1938 Pontiac six is surrounded by two smacked-up Chevys. You can see the 1931 Chevrolet taillamp in foreground and a 1947 Chevrolet coupe in the background. It looks like the Pontiac hit a sign advertising Crystal Cave, Pa., a tourist attraction located between Allentown and Reading. When driving antique autos, avoid becoming an "accidental tourist." (Frank Malatesta Collection)

Buick built 79,510 of these 1938 Special four-door Touring Sedans for sale here, plus 2,681 others for export. When new, this car sold for $1,047 (or less than 50¢ per pound). Photo of this smashed up example was snapped in January (note canvas radiator cover) of 1941. Don't limit your "special" driving to modern cars; old cars need careful operation as well! (Frank Malatesta Collection)

About $18 worth of labor and $5.80 for a new runningboard assembly would have put this 1938 Chevrolet five-window coupe back in good condition. Note the single fog lamp and accessory center grille guard. Judging from New Jersey license plates, the car was nearly new when it was dented. (Frank Malatesta Collection)

Ford built just 2,703 Model 81A convertible sedans in 1938. Here's one that probably missed becoming a collector's car because another vehicle didn't miss hitting it head-on. Don't miss a beat when driving your Early V-8 Ford! (Frank Malatesta Collection)

This car looks like a 1939 Buick Limited Touring Sedan, but we can't tell if it's the six- or eight-passenger version. Both were rare cars, with production runs of 382 and 686 units (domestic and export) in respective order. In addition, 543 limousines were built in this series. (Frank Malatesta Collection)

After sealed beam headlamps were introduced in 1940, the automotive aftermarket made replacement sealed beam headlamps for older model cars. This 1939 Nash sedan has a pair installed. The car has only minor accident damage, but the interior was totally gutted by a fire. Don't smoke while driving your antique auto — ashes can cause fires! (Frank Malatesta Collection)

Little Falls Laundry, of Red Bank, N.J., owned this 1940 Ford sedan delivery and identified it as vehicle no. 93 in the firm's fleet. This now-very-desirable light commercial vehicle took a hit on the left-hand door, runningboard and rear fender. Note broken windshield and shattered door glass. (Frank Malatesta Collection)

Impact from a moderate crash pushed in the rear fender of this 1941 Ford sedan delivery on May 21, 1942. When new, this model sold for $746. Its "book value" was around $690, when this damage occurred. Stay alert behind the wheel of your antique car! (Frank Malatesta Collection)

This poor 1940 Buick came through World War II usage in fine shape, only to wind up a target for a tree blown over during a 1951 windstorm. Damage such as this might be fixed today, but it's likely this car — worth under $200 at the time — was simply sold to a scrapyard. John W. Gorman took the photo.

Undated accident photo shows a 1939 Packard coupe which took down a picket fence and hit a house in California. It seems to have missed the utility pole, however. The photo is part of a collection which the National Motor Museum of Great Britain purchased in Los Angeles some years ago. (Courtesy National Motor Museum, Beaulieu, Hants, England)

It looks like someone attempted some amateur hammer and dolly work on the damaged fender of a 1940 Packard five-window coupe. What appears to be a homemade trailer is being pulled behind the old Packard in this photo snapped in 1947 (Peter F. Zierden)

This 1940 Ford Standard Tudor sedan has dents here and there all over its body. The grille center (but not the grille guard) is pushed in, the left front fender has a dimple, the hubcap is dinged and the driver's door is distorted. Don't let your antique Ford wind up in an accident; drive safely! (Frank Malatesta Collection)

Here's a wreck that any restorer would love to get his hands on today! The 1940 Ford Deluxe convertible seems to have slid into another object on a wet, icy roadway. However, the damage is not extensive. Elmer Nordness, of the Madison, Wis., Water Utility snapped the photo in 1941 and Jim Kelly sent it to "Wreck of the Week."

Hubcap design suggest that this wrecked touring car is a Packard of about 1914-1915 vintage. It took a lot of force to bend that front bumper like that. Don't bump into anything with your antique car!

Ted Cook, of Spring Lake, N.J., was in the coal business from 1929 to 1959. His trucks made regular runs from Scranton, Pa. to Neptune, N.J. This 1940 Dodge tractor was one of several rigs that had bad experiences on the road. Truck collectors take note and "keep on truckin'" safely.

Do you think the owner of this 1940 Dodge sedan would have driven a bit more carefully, if he knew that World War II was going to halt the production lines and make cars very scarce? Photo dates from March 1941. Join the war on old car accidents by driving antique autos extra-carefully! (Frank Malatesta Collection)

The 1947 New Jersey license plates suggest that is the year this 1940 Oldsmobile ragtop was rear-ended. Note chrome exhaust deflector, right-hand rearview mirror and curb guide on front fender, as well as wide range of years and type of vehicles parked nearby. Street cleaner seems to have taken the day off! Help curb unsafe hobby touring by practicing safe driving habits. (Frank Malatesta Collection)

That rare front bumper guard was designed to protect this equally rare 1941 Oldsmobile woodie station wagon from damage, but failed. There is a badge at the rear of the hood announcing that this car featured "Olds Hydramatic" drive. Make safety and "automatic" habit, when driving your antique Olds! (Frank Malatesta Collection)

Here's a look at the passenger side of a hard-to-find 1941 Oldsmobile "woodie" station wagon, which was wrecked in a bad accident. It's hard to say if parts were damaged by crash or used to repair a similar car. (Frank Malatesta Collection)

A gaping hole has been poked in the passenger door of this new-looking 1941 Oldsmobile sedan. The car has several interesting options and accessories, including Hydramatic Drive ($100 extra); fog lamps ($10.00 per pair); bumper guards ($3.75 each) and a hard-to-find grille guard. (Frank Malatesta Collection)

It looks like this 1941 Buick Special sedanette has already been given its "junkyard" number. The 1945 Illinois license plate indicates when the car was wrecked. Notice the Dodge in front of the Buick. It has Chevy-type bumper ends. The accident took place at 63rd Street and Indiana, in an unidentified Illinois city. Photo is from the Randy Fleischhauer Collection.

Head-on collision folded up the front of this 1941 Studebacker as if it were an accordian. The car has the white plastic trim rings used to give a wide whiteall look just after the war, when conventional white sidewall tires weren't available. Drive your Studebaker like a safety champion! (Frank Malatesta Collection)

This partially up-ended 1942 Chevy slammed into a 1940 Plymouth on a California street. License plates date the photo to 1949. It's hard to determine how the Chevy wound up like this with damage shown. This print comes from a collection purchased by the National Motor Museum of Beaulieu, England.

This new Chrysler had a wreck on March 27, 1942. Strangely, the bumper and grille are hardly scraped, but the upper fenders and hood took a real licking. Some late-1942 Chryslers had painted "blackout" trim, so this car must have been built early in the abbreviated model-year. Careful cruising in your Chryslers! (Frank Malatesta Collection.)

Pontiac dealer wound up taking in this 1942 Plymouth after it was damaged. At first glance, the car looks like it was in a minor fender-bender. However, a closer look at the shape of the roof suggests that more severe damage exists. Drive your Plymouth carefully! (Frank Malatesta Collection)

Plastic "whitewall" disks seem to show up more on Chrysler products than on other types of cars. This 1947 Dodge sedan has them. Extensive frontal damage occurred to the left side of this vehicle in a New Jersey accident, just after World War II. (Frank Malatesta Collection)

Close-up photo shows heaviest damage to right rear fender of this 1947 DeSoto. Since the New Jersey license plates were issued the same year, we can assume this is a practically new automobile that doesn't belong to Richie Cunningham's dad! Drive your vintage DeSoto carefully and you'll have "Happy Days." (Frank Malatesta Collection)

This 1947 Dodge might have been written off as a total wreck, after it was involved in a collision that severely damaged the front right-hand corner of the car. We're sure that some MoPar fan would love to find and restore it today. Put the "dodge" on antique car accidents; stay alert when touring the highways! (Frank Malatesta Collection)

An accident occurring in 1948 tore up the passenger side of this 1947 Plymouth. Look how the plastic wheel trim ring was twisted and torn by the force of the collision. Be careful when you "ship out" in your Plymouth! (Frank Malatesta Collection)

The Wisconsin license plates on this banged-up 1947-1948 Mercury have an August 1954 validation tab. The photo sent in by James L. Gwaltney, of Anderson, Ind., emphasizes the danger of driving at night. It should serve as a reminder that your hobby cars be equipped properly for after-dark use with all headlamps and taillights in good working order.

This Chevrolet school bus was damaged in a California accident in the late 1940s. The police car appears to be a 1947-1948 Ford with round parking lamps below its headlights. Firefighters are flushing oil or gas from the roadway, which would not be done in this manner today, due to increased concern for the enviornment. (Courtesy of the National Motor Museum, Beaulieu, Hants, England.)

Don Servais, of Maumee, Ohio, photographed accidents for the Ohio State Patrol from 1948 to 1962. This wreck took place May 8, 1948 at 8:15 a.m., at the intersection of Broadway and Allen Street in Don's hometown. It involved a Dodge stake truck and an old Chevrolet. Remember, all of us have a "stake" in old car hobby safety!

Cadillac built only 3,100 Series 62 convertible coupes in 1941 and here is one that never became a collector's car. The accident took place in the mid-1950s, when ragtops such as this one were considered only "used cars." (The Randy Fleischhauer Collection)

According to H.G. Jacobson, of Long Beach, Calif., this wreck happened in Puerto Rico sometime in 1945. The driver hit a utility pole with his military vehicle, but exact details concerning the accident aren't available.

"Mr. Ed," of Baraboo, Wis, sent in this snapshot. The 51-year-old driver of the car was injured when a Milwaukee Road train carried the vehicle along the railroad tracks after the car skidded into it. This took place on Dec. 18, 1948 15 7:40 p.m. The car is a 1941 Chevrolet coupe.

This Chrysler convertible flipped off a Montana highway and landed upside down in the ditch alongside the road. Will Byersdorff, of Menomonee Falls, Wis. snapped the picture. Chrysler fans who appreciate the rarity of this car should get a safe driving message from this photo.

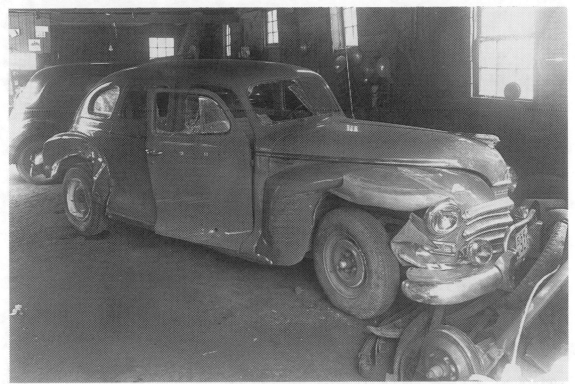

This 1947 Plymouth has current issue New Jersey license tags, suggesting that it was wrecked by a careless motorist who had little respect for new automobiles. Perhaps he was driving the prewar Ford in the background. Wonder what cars those hubcaps hanging on wall of repair shop fit? "Holy hubcaps! Driving old cars as if they were the Batmobile can make you a real wreck!" (Frank Malatesta Collection)

Apparently, the fire department in a New Jersey city used this Plymouth as a chief's car immediately after the war. We'd guess that it took off on an emergency run and caused a second emergency before it arrived. Remember, if you drive your old car like a fire truck you may wind up getting burned! (Frank Malatesta Collection)

Accident photographer was on the scene when a Dodge dump truck ran into a 1947 Hudson sedan on the streets of Paterson, N.J. The 1951 Mercury across the intersection appears to be a station wagon. Coming up the street behind it is an old-fashioned city bus. Police officer looks more interested in posing for camera than directing traffic. (Frank Malatesta Collection)

Trying to figure out what type of accident caused specific types of damage can be difficult. This 1948 Lincoln, for example, has a scraped front fender, dented door post, damaged rear wheel cover and is missing a portion of its rear quarter trim molding. Drive your Lincoln safely! (Frank Malatesta Collection)

This wreck demolished the front end of a 1947 Cadillac 62 sedan. Notice the accessory spotlamp and outside sun visor. Rectangular front fog lamps were also optional equipment. This car is one of 25,834 built. Photo by James W. Seymour from the Randy Fleischhauer Collection)

Smashed-up 1947 Chevrolet has a different "slant" on life, following a severe front end collision. The four-passenger coupe looks like it was in real good shape before the accident. However, it probably wound up in a salvage yard, rather than a body repair shop. It is a Stylemaster model. (Frank Malatesta Collection)

The owner of this 1947 Chevrolet Stylemaster Sport Coupe probably won't be putting any more Calso Supreme gasoline in its tank, even though the fuel was "skyway blended for highway power." Chevy made 34,513 of these cars and priced them at $1,202. Note the chrome trim rings, which are getting hard to find today. (Frank Malatesta Collection)

Banged-up 1947 Pontiac Streamliner six suffered massive damage in this Illinois night-time accident. This car originally sold for $1,407, but it sure wasn't worth much in this shape. (Photo by James W. Seymour from the Randy Fleischhauer Collection)

This looks like a Plymouth collector's worst nightmare. The Diamond Reo dump truck couldn't stop in time and plowed into the 1946-1948 Plymouth sedan at relatively high velocity. Note the 1950 Ford police car used by the Algonquin, Ill. gendarmes. (Photo by James W. Seymour from the Randy Fleischhauer collection)

Here's a revealing view of what can happen when a Diamond Reo dump truck rear-ends a 1947 Plymouth sedan. Although the driver's compartment remained fairly intact, it was instantly air conditioned. Note the 1950 Ford Illinois police car. (Randy Fleischhauer Collection)

Luckily, this photo doesn't depict members of the Oldsmobile Club of America on their way to a convention. It's from the mid-1950s and shows a sun-visored 1947 Oldsmobile sedanette which was clobbered by a 1954 Oldsmobile 88 coupe. The crash occurred in Illinois. (The Randy Fleischhauer Collection)

This 1948 Packard Super Eight sedan collided with a late 1940s truck in the Los Angeles area, when both vehicles were nearly new. Photo courtesy of Earle C. Anthony Region of The Packard Club, provided by Stuart Blond, of Fords, N.J.

Here's how a 1948 Mercury looks after flipping through the air and crashing into a state patrol car on U.S. 12, east of Paw-Paw, Mich, in 1952 or 1953. After the impact, the convertible slid backwards, on its passenger side, into a cemetary. The driver wound up with only scratches on his cheek and a bump on his head from a door that slammed back shut as he was exiting the car. (H.R. "Skip" Strong)

The driver of this 1948 Mercury convertible escaped the accident, which wrecked his rag-top, with minor injuries. The car crossed over the centerline, hit a semi-truck, became air-borne, rolled twice in the air and slammed into a state patrol car! (Courtesy H.R. "Skip" Strong)

Terry Lee Chandler, of Lainesburg, Mich., missed a curve and wrecked his 1947 Chevrolet street rod on June 26, 1985. Terry Wagner, who sent the photo, said that Chandler was out of a hospital and doing well by Aug. 1985. Highway safety is a "hot" concern of the old car hobby's modified branch.

Picture shows an English "breakdown patrol" attending to an accident which occurred in the 1950s. Upside down car is an English Ford. Courtesy of the National Motor Museum, Beaulieu, Hants, England)

Around 1948, the English auto-maker Austin made a strong effort to market its products in the U.S. This A40 Somerset sedan was owned by a member of the North Jersey Automobile Club who had to use his towing insurance after he had a crash. The 1949 accident inflicted rear end damage. It looks like that tow truck hauled the little car to an Austin dealership. (Frank Malatesta Collection)

With production of 32,392 units, the 1949 Chevrolet convertible isn't exactly a rare car, but that's no reason to drive one into a snowbank. Actually, this example wound up that way, following an accident in Illinois. (James W. Seymour photo from The Randy Fleischhauer Collection)

This accident brought two old cars together with a bang in 1958, according to Randy Fleischhauer, who sent us the photo. The cars appear to be a 1947 Nash four-door sedan and a 1949 Styleline coupe. When hobbyists talk about old car "meets," this is not what they mean!

California fog or smog may have been a contributing factor in the dramatic wreck of a 1954 MG-TF roadster and a 1950 Chevrolet Styleline sedan. Obviously, the smaller sports car came out on the bottom in this accident. Note the old wrecker and the fire truck with a Dalmatian on its hose bed. When driving your old car, always take weather conditions into account. The National Motor Museum of Great Britain supplied this photograph.

A vehicle skidding on a snowy road hit and wrecked this 1950 Chevrolet Styleline four-door sedan. Before the accident, this was a pretty dressed-up "Stovebolt," with a plastic bug deflector on its hood, a steering wheel cover, an outside sun visor and fender skirts. (Photo by James W. Seymour from the Randy Fleischhauer Collection)

According to photographer Andy Dressel, of Bethal Park, Pa., this 1949 Pontiac Stream-liner 8 two-door sedan hit a utility pole in the South Hills section of Pittsburgh during 1955. We hope that all antique Pontiac fans will make safe driving one of their "chief" concerns.

"Mr. Ed," of Baraboo, Wis., provided this photo of a Plymouth convertible that was wrecked in Sauk County on Jan. 21, 1956. The MoPar ragtop, complete with spotlamp and fog lights, was totaled by a truck. The accident took place at 10:15 p.m. and makes a good case for careful nighttime driving.

Crowded city streets have always provided motorists with lots of hazzards to watch for. In this case, the driver of a 1949 Pontiac failed to use care when making a turn and entered a one-way street traveling in the wrong direction. When making antique car tours in a city, keep your eyes peeled in all directions. (Frank Malatesta Collection)

Despite loss of back window, the roof of this 1949 Mercury four-door sedan stayed structually intact during a dramatic roll-over. Photo was taken by Northern Illinois accident photographer James W. Seymour. (Courtesy The Randy Fleischhauer Collection)

This Willys-Jeep pickup truck was wrecked on Feb. 8, 1956. It belonged to Bernard Bell Fence Supplies, of Algonquin, Ill. The wet highway was probably a contributing factor in the accident, which happened on Route 176 west of Highway 31. (James W. Seymour photo courtesy of The Randy Fleischhauer Collection)

Woman uses gestures to try to explain what caused the wreck of a 1949 Ford Fordor sedan which wound up with moderately heavy sheet metal damage. Crash took place Sept. 29, 1957 on Route 31 in Illinois. (James W. Seymour photo from The Randy Fleischhauer Collection)

You don't see many 1949 Oldsmobile convertibles today, but this one may have survived to become a collector's car. It suffered only minor front fender damage in a crash that took place May 5, 1955 at the corner of Route 14 and Lake Street in Crystal Lake, Ill. (The Randy Fleischhauer Collection)

Judging by its cab styling, this Model L International "Roadliner" tractor could be a 1950-1952 model. Its new one-piece windshield stayed in one piece when it jack-knifed on a slippery roadway. Photo was snapped by accident photograher James W. Seymour, of Crystal Lake, Ill. (Courtesy The Randy Fleischhauer Collection)

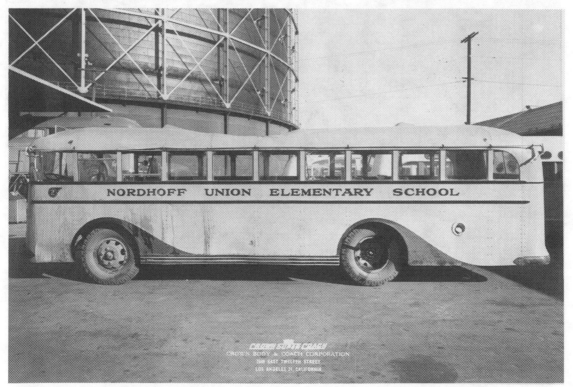

This accident-damaged bus was built by the Crown Body and Coach Corp. of Los Angeles, Calif. It seems to have overturned on its right side, causing damage to the roof and fracturing several windows. Commercial vehicle historian Don Wood sent the photo as a big safety message for old vehicle hobbyists.

Professor Don Wood sent in this dramatic photo of a school bus that turned over after sliding off the road, near a fruit orchard in California, in the early postwar years. The high school and junior college students who rode the vehicle were lucky this happened when it was empty.

Pontiac offered its 1950 convertible in Chieftain Deluxe form only. However, buyers could select between six- or eight-cylinder inline flathead engines. This car has a "Silver-8-Streak" badge on its battered left-hand fender. Notice that there is even more extensive sheet metal damage to the rear. Drive your Pontiac safely! (Randy Flauchbauer Collection)

This crash took place in the 1950s at an unknown location. It involved a 1955 Buick Riviera hardtop and a 1955 Chevrolet Bel Air sedan. Photo courtesy of Leonard Misuraca, a member of the Packards East Region of The Packard Club. Provided by Stuart Blond.

A 1952 Buick Special wound up in a ditch after sideswiping a 1950 Ford. The smaller car is dolled up with a bug deflector, headlamp eyebrows, a sun visor, fender skirts, mud flaps and a rear antenna. Don't "ditch" safety just because you're driving a collector car! (Randy Fleischhauer Collection)

This photo shows something rare . . . three cars of the same year involved in a single accident. From left to right, they are a 1951 Plymouth, a 1951 Studebaker and a 1951 Buick Roadmaster. The picture was snapped by James W. Seymour, a Crystal Lake, Ill. car buff who specialized in taking accident photos. (Courtesy The Randy Fleischhauer Collection)

This old car — we think it's a 1951 Studebaker — was heavily damaged in a collision that occurred during 1958. Randy Fleischhauer, of Mesa, Ariz., sent in the photo.

Heavy damage was inflicted to the rear end of this Buick in an early postwar accident. It's a 1950 Roadmaster Deluxe Riviera four-door sedan with the sweep spear trim introduced in the middle of that model year. Be the master of the road when driving antique cars; drive carefully! (The Randy Fleischhauer Collection)

A 1952 Dodge and a 1950 Buick bounced into each other during a rainstorm in Illinois. The driver of a 1954 Oldsmobile 98 stopped to "rubberneck" the accident scene. Drive your post-war cars safely! (Randy Fleischhauer Collection)

Jim D. Jones, of Cincinnati, Ohio, reports that this Plymouth was totaled when a 1954 Buick ran a stop sign and hit it hard. The accident took place May 3, 1959 on State Road 49 north of Dayton. It reminds us that hobbyists should lock all doors when driving their antique cars.

This 1949 Ford was a victim of a storm that swept through St. Paul, Minn. in 1951, causing extensive wind damage and knocking over many large trees. It looks like someone took very good care of the car before this happened. Thanks to John W. Gorman, of Minneapolis, for the dramatic photo.

This tree, knocked over by heavy winds in a St. Paul, Minn. storm, seems to have preferred Kaisers to Fords. It came down on the hood of a 1951 Deluxe Tudor sedan, totally wrecking the front of the vehicle, while a Kaiser parked across the street appears undamaged. John Gorman photo.

The term "flathead" Ford doesn't mean anything like this! A windstorm that blew through St. Paul, Minn., in 1951, caused the wreckage of this Ford. It was a new car at the time. John W. Gorman's photo should inspire old car lovers to keep their cars inside the garage during heavy storm warnings.

John Gorman, of Minneapolis, Minn., took a series of wrecked car photos following a heavy windstorm that hit the city of St. Paul during 1951. This sidemounted 1933-1934 sedan was heavily damaged when the storm toppled a big tree on its roof. It would be a good parts car today.

Randy Fleischhauer sent this photo of a 1951 Ford Custom Deluxe Victoria which wound up in a ditch after a nighttime collision. The car is one of 110,286 two-door hardtops that Ford manufactured in that model's first year on the market. It does not appear to be too extensively damaged, but is very dirty.

Photographer Andy Dressel, of Bethal Park, Pa., had a friend who owned a police radio. He would call Andy whenever he heard reports of an accident over the police band. One of the wrecks Andy responded to was a 1950 Dodge truck that crashed, during 1955, in the South Hills section of Pittsburgh.

Photographer Bill Tucker's parents were lucky to escape being hurt in an early 1960s accident which totaled their 1952 DeSoto. "A very nice car was destroyed," he advised. "The insurance company replaced it with a 1952 DeSoto two-door hardtop, which was never as good as the four-door sedan."

William Tucker sent photos of a 1952 DeSoto four-door sedan which his parents were driving near Indianapolis in 1960 or 1961. They met a flatbed truck hauling a bulldozer that had slipped sideways, causing the blade to stick out. Bill's stepfather saw the danger. He pushed his wife against the right-hand door of their car and then laid down on the seat, preventing injuries to both of them.

Both left-hand doors of this 1950 Plymouth took a direct hit in a vehicle accident. Note that there was actually very little structural damage, proving the sturdiness of Chrysler's box-on-box styling. Drive your Plymouth safely! (Frank Malatesta Collection)

When Chevy trucks with windows were known as Carry-Alls, Plymouth station wagons were called Suburbans. This 1951 Concord Suburban was heavily damaged in a nighttime accident which occurred in Illinois in the mid-'50s. Accident and safety photographer James W. Seymour took the picture. (Courtesy The Randy Fleischhauer Collection)

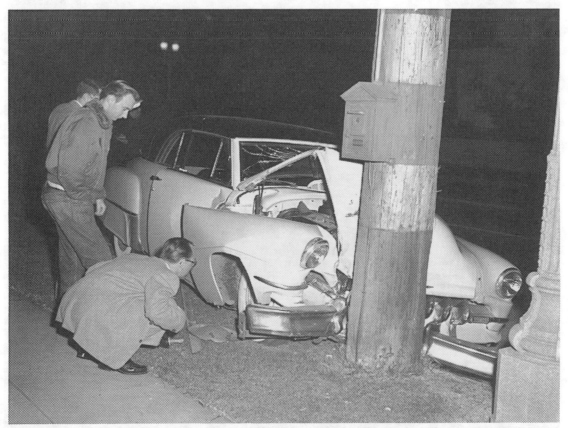

Utility poles and 1951 DeSoto Sportsman hardtops don't mix well together. The dressy MoPar had wide whitewall tires, full wheel disks and fender skirts. Do you think the impact set off the fire alarm box? This accident took place in the Los Angeles, Calif. area. (Courtesy National Motor Museum, Beaulieu, Hants, England)

License plate tag indicates that this New York-based 1951 Chrysler sedan was rear-ended in 1952. Whatever caused the damage only grazed the rear bumper, but gave the deck lid a solid impact! Note the 1941 Buick and 1940 Plymouth parked nearby. Drive your Chrysler carefully! (Frank Malatesta Collection)

A hot iron might take the crease off this photo, but the creases in the 1951 Ford are there to stay. Impact ripped a hole in the top of the left front fender. Notice the sticker placed on the windshield by the accident investigation squad. (Randy Fleischhauer Collection)

It almost seems that 1949-1951 Fords were particularly susceptible to wrecks, since we have obtained so many photos of damaged examples. Here's a 1951 Custom Tudor Sedan which was hit hard enough on the right-hand front fender to damage both the hood and grille. Notice the broken headlamp. (James W. Seymour photo from the Randy Fleischhauer Collection)

Pontiac commemorated its 25th anniversary during 1951 and this Chieftain DeLuxe four-door sedan seems to have over-celebrated the milestone. Like many Pontiacs of this era, this one has several factory accessories including a front master grille guard, spotlight and outside sun visor. (James W. Seymour photo from the Randy Fleischhauer Collection)

It seems that this 1951 Kaiser two-door sedan was involved in a rollover. Notice the dirty hubcaps. Apparently, the ground was soft enough to keep the damage relatively light. Less than 1,500 cars of this body style were built by Kaiser in two series, so this is a relatively rare machine. Drive your Kaiser and your Fraser safely! (Frank Malatesta Collection)

This "ram-tough" Dodge was rammed into something big enough to bend it up pretty badly. It looks like a 1951 Wayfarer model and, judging from the New Jersey license plates, the wreck took place when it was one-year-old. Drive your Dodge carefully! (Frank Malatesta Collection)

Anyone who thinks that the Vega was Chevy's first three-door model shouldn't be fooled by the fact that this 1952 Styleline Deluxe sedan has only three doors left after an accident. Note the 1954 Chevrolet full-wheel disks. Drive your Chevy in style; safety style, that is! (The Randy Fleischhauer Collection)

Small hubcaps look unusual on a fancy 1952 Pontiac Catalina Deluxe, which ran into a 1951 Studebaker Champion six sedan. Damage to the Pontiac seems worst, even though it was the larger, heavier vehicle. Accident took place May 21, 1957 on Route 176 in McHenry County, Ill. (James W. Seymour photo from the Randy Fleischhauer Collection)

Remember relective red tape being used to decorate cars during the 1950s? This 1951 Studebaker has it on the rear bumper and trunk. An unusual addition to the 1952 Pontiac Catalina is the aftermarket stoplamps mounted to the bumper. (James W. Seymour photo from the Randy Fleischhauer Collection)

A vintage tow truck hauls away a 1952 Mercury Custom two-door sedan that suffered fairly extensive front end damage in a nighttime collision. The handsome Merc — one of only 25,812 built — has whitewall tires and factory fender skirts. Randy Fleischhauer, of Mesa, Ariz., provided the photo.

"We have to stop meeting like this!" Maybe that's what the owner of this 1952 Ford said to the driver of the 1954 Packard when they bumped into each other at an Illinois intersection. Drive your old car extra carefully when it's wet outside! (Randy Fleischhauer Collection)

When this accident took place on Aug. 24. 1957, this 1953 Chevy Bel Air convertible suffered a smashed fender. Originally selling for $2,093, the ragtop had an average retail value of around $710 just before it was wrecked. (The Randy Fleischhauer Collection)

Pontiac versus Ford was not limited to Daytona stock car racing in the 1960s. This 1953 Pontiac two-door sedan and 1964 Ford hardtop slugged it out on a snowy Illinois highway. Notice that the ambulance in front of the older car is also a Pontiac which would be very collectible today. (James W. Seymour photo from the Randy Fleischhauer Collection)

The end of the road for this 1954 Oldsmobile 88 two-door hardtop came after a multi-car collision that damaged both the front and rear end of the vehicle. Photo contributed by Randy Fleischhauer shows the car being hooked to a wrecker, which hauled it away to an auto graveyard.

Slick roadways following snowfalls have always compromised motor vehicle safety. This 1953 Pontiac Chieftain Deluxe four-door sedan couldn't stop quick enough to avoid an accident. Notice the 1956 Plymouth police cars. (James W. Seymour photo from the Randy Fleischhauer Collection)

Badly damaged 1953 Pontiac Chieftain Deluxe four-door sedan was probably a candidate for the salvage yard after this brutal wreck. Although the car suffered extensive sheet metal damage, passenger compartment integrity seems to be pretty solid. The photo comes from the Randy Fleischhauer Collection.

Illinois "Land of Lincoln" license plates on front of 1953 Ford suggest that the car had its "lights poked out" in a 1964 accident in that state. Also damaged was the right front fender and grille. (James W. Seymour photo from the Randy Fleischhauer Collection)

This two-car accident involved a 1953 Ford Customline four-door sedan, of which 374,487 were made, and a 1955 Plymouth Belvedere two-door hardtop, which was one of 47,375 built. Neither car in the photo sent by Randy Fleischhauer looks too heavily damaged to be repaired.

This 1954 Cadillac 60 Special four-door sedan was involved in some type of accident that damaged the passenger side sheet metal, rear door frame and roof of the vehicle. The photo is from the Randy Fleischhauer Collection.

Ford Motor Co. built 44,315 two-door Ranch Wagons in 1954. This V-8 powered example lasted only one year. It was wrecked after colliding with a tree in Mount Lebanon, Pa. during 1955. The little girl sucking her pinky doesn't seem to fazed by the excitement. Andy Dressel snapped the picture.

Check out the ambulance which responded to this crash of a 1953 DeSoto four-door sedan and a 1955 Chevrolet half-ton pickup truck. It's a Chevrolet professional vehicle — probably built by Superior Coach — with Impala style trim on its rear quarters. (James W. Seymour photo courtesy of The Randy Fleischhauer Collection)

A truck hit this 1954 Chevy broadside on June 8, 1960, heavily damaging the entire front end of the Bel Air four-door sedan. The accident occurred near Granville, Ohio, on state road 16. Jim D. Jones sent in the photo. Keep your antique cars out of the path of speeding trucks!

The rear door of this 1954 Chevrolet 210 sedan received a slight bump. The right-hand parking lamp housing is also damaged. In the background is a 1955 Bel Air hardtop and a 1951 Studebaker. The Chevrolet has 1958 New Jersey license plates. (Frank Malatesta Collection)

This photo was taken in New Jersey in the late 1950s. Two 1957 Chevys appear in reflections on the service station windows. The car is a 1954 Pontiac Custom Star Chief Catalina, which took a real slam on its front right-hand side. It should inspire Pontiac lovers to drive more carefully.

This Buick wound up next to a Ford across from a Chrysler dealership, while a 1951 Pontiac ambulamnce came to take the driver to a medical facility. The car is one of 31,919 Century four-door sedans built during model-year 1954. (James W. Seymour photo from the Randy Fleischhauer Collection)

Old Cars Weekly *Research Editor Ken Buttolph survived the crash that totaled his 1954 Kaiser years ago. During the accident, in New London, Wis., Ken ducked under the instrument panel and held on to the steering column for dear life. Today, he has an identical Kaiser which looks like this one did before the wreck.*

Full wheel disks and whitewalls cost extra on this 1954 Pontiac Chieftain Special two-door sedan. This car cost only $2,027 when it was new. However, it was worth a lot less after hitting the concrete abutment. (James W. Seymour photo from the Randy Fleischhauer Collection)

This 1954 Ford Customline, with 1955 Illinois license plates, was probably just a year old when it rolled over and flipped through a barbed wire fence. The script on the deck lid tells us that the four-door sedan was equipped with optional overdrive. Drive your postwar Ford safely! (James W. Seymour photo from the Randy Fleischhauer Collection)

English Ford Squire station wagon slammed into a 1954 Oldsmobile two-door sedan in a California street sometime after 1958. Notice the "wood" trim on the compact wagon's door. (Courtesy National Motor Museum of Great Britain, Beaulieu, Hants, England)

The sign says "stop," but this 1955 Plymouth kept on going ...and crashed. The car that it hit was a big 1953 Chrysler. It looks as if the crowd has decided to hang around and watch the tow truck do its job. Drive your postwar MoPars carefully! (James W. Seymour photo from the Randy Fleischhauer Collection)

Rain may have contributed to the crash which wrecked this 1955 Ford Fairlane Victoria two-door hardtop. Note the fuzzy dice, Mercury cruiser skirts and "spinners" added to the stock Ford wheel disks. Don't make your "Vicky" an accident victim, drive it carefully! (James W. Seymour photo from the Randy Fleischhauer Collection)

According to Phil Campbell, a sociology professor at the University of Minnesota, this 1955 Chevrolet Bel Air was owned by a young man in Duluth who purchased it, not too long ago, and drove it regularly until he had a "jousting match" with one of his friends. We hope he had it fully insured.

Professor Philip Campbell entitled this photo "You're Out." He said, "There's a touch of sadness in that the '55 Chevy made it 30 years, only to be wiped out in a crash. At least, so to speak, it died with its boots on!" The photo proves that accidents involving older cars still occur today.

This 1955 Chevy 210 looks very similar to the first car that the editor of this book ever owned. I wonder if it has the same Delray interior? The car's rear fender is crunched and the rear deck lid is smashed. Do you think this classic Chevy was repaired? Drive your post-war Chevy carefully! (James W. Seymour photo from the Randy Fleischhauer Collection)

Classic Chevys — such as this 1955 One-Fifty — made good police cars when equipped with the "small-block" 265 cid overhead valve V-8. They were light and fast — sometimes too fast for the law enforcement officers to handle. This one slid off the road, spilling oil and antifreeze everywhere. (James W. Seymour photo from the Randy Fleischhauer Collection)

How many Classic Chevy Collectors would use a zebra-striped steering wheel cover? The 1955 Bel Air hardtop (185,562 built) was hit by a much rarer (2,000 built) 1954 Dodge Royal convertible. This accident occurred Feb. 17, 1956 on Route 58 near Elgin, Ill. (James W. Seymour photo from the Randy Fleischhauer Collection)

Passing on two-lane rural highways, even on straight patches of road, can lead to accidents. This one put a 1952 Plymouth in the ditch and caused a 1955 Pontiac sedan to block one entire lane. When you're antique car touring, suppress the urge to pass up slower tourers! (James W. Seymour photo via The Randy Fleischhauer Collection)

Photographer Andy Dressel, of Bethel Park, Pa., captured this two-car accident on film, in Mt. Lebanon, Pa., during 1955. The car on the left is a 1949 DeSoto and the telephone pole was enough to bring the new Oldsmobile to an abrupt halt. Excessive speed was probably a factor in this collision and should be avoided whenever driving a postwar antique car today.

This 1955 Oldsmobile has a "Holiday" front fender script, indicating that it is the two-door hardtop model. It seems to have mounted the curb, side-swiped a 1949 DeSoto and impacted a utility pole. The wreck occurred in Mt. Lebanon, Pa. in 1955 and Andy Dressel took the picture.

This 1955 Oldsmobile Super 88 flipped over on a grass embankment. We wonder if the wreck happened while trying to elude the 1956 Ford police car in the background? The roof of the vehicle appears to have been strong enough to support it on the grass embankment. Photo comes from Randy Fleischhauer.

This 1955 Olds 88 Holiday Coupe would probably be restored quickly today, since its accident damage is relatively minor. Note the 1956 Dodge with dual exhausts parked nearby) (James W. Seymour photo from the Randy Fleischhauer Collection)

A wrecker tows away a 1955 Olds 88 Holiday Coupe which ran into another car at this intersection. Highway patrol officer gathers eyewitness details, while passengers gawk at the nice condition of the car. Note that another 1955 Olds is parked nearby. (James W. Seymour photo from the Randy Fleischhauer Collection)

Two 1960 cars — a Pontiac hardtop and a Dodge station wagon — flank this accident-damaged 1955 Buick. With close to or more than 200 hp in all models, Buicks of this era were much quicker than the old straight eights, which led to some spectacular crashes. (James W. Seymour photo from the Randy Fleischhauer Collection)

Today's firefighters probably would not go up to an overturned car without donning full protective gear. Hey fellows, that leak could be gasoline! The car, a 1955 Buick Century Riviera Sedan, looks to be a total loss. (Courtesy National Motor Museum, Beaulieu, England)

At least the owner of this 1955 Cadillac picked a spot nearby a surgical appliance store to have his accident. The General Motors luxury car, which appears nearly new, took out a parking meter along with the backside of a 1951 Pontiac. (Courtesy National Motor Museum, Beaulieu, England)

Snowstorms are a major cause of motor vehicle accidents in the United States. In this one, a 1956 Cadillac Coupe DeVille knocked the hood right off a 1952 Buick Special, which wound up in the ditch. Most collector cars aren't driven in snow, but if they are, extra care should be used. (The Randy Fleischhauer Collection)

Relatively few of the wreck photos we've seen show 1956 Chevys. Here's one that slid off the road after being hit in the left front fender. Note the dent in the roof and missing windshield. Drive your '56 Chevy safely! (James W. Seymour photo from the Randy Fleischhauer Collection)

That tire pump on the ground may have been used to fix a flat caused by this accident, which wrecked a 1956 Mercury Custom two-door hardtop. This is a rather rare car, since only 20,857 were made. They listed for $2,485 when new. Drive your postwar Mercury safely! (James W. Seymour photo from the Randy Fleischhauer Collection)

One evening, when George Peltier was working for a northern Michigan newspaper as a photographer, he drove past the local Ford-Mercury-Lincoln dealership and saw this heart-stopping scene. He later heard that a truck crane was used to lift up the new 1956 Lincoln so the ramps could be straightened.

Jim D. Jones of Cincinnati sent this photo of a 1956 Ford Customline two-door sedan (one of 164,828 built), which rolled over on State Road 73 near Wilmington, Ohio. When the accident occurred on Valentine's Day 1963, this car was worth below $345 at retail and had a loan value below $175.

This 1956 Ford Fairlane Victoria belonged to Chip Miller, one of the organizers of the giant swap meets held in Carlisle, Pa., by the Flea Marketeers. Bob Lichty, who handles publicity for the shows, sent the pictures. Lichty advises that the wreck took place in 1960, near Chip's home in Jenkintown, Pa.

Ford Motor Co. built 42,317 of these 1956 Custom Ranch Wagons. This example of the relatively rare two-door station wagon was wrecked in a 1958 accident. At the time, it was worth $940-1,470 at cash value and $1,410 - 1,560 at retail. Randy Fleischhauer forwarded the photo to **Old Cars Weekly**.

A 15-year-old driver rolled this 1956 DeSoto Fireflite four-door Sportsman over on a county road near Pataskala, Ohio on May 4, 1965. The car was one of only 3,350 four-door hardtops that DeSoto built in the model's first year. The photo was sent in by Jim D. Jones, of Cincinnati.

Heeding stop signs is a basic law of safe driving and the owner of this 1956 Oldsmobile learned, the hard way, what happens when the law is broken. In 1957, a front fender for this car cost $41.25; a hood top panel sold for $57.50; a complete set of bumper components was $164.85 and painting and undercoating was additional. John G. Linhardt, of Jamaica, N.Y., sent the photo.

Everyone involved in this fender-bender between a 1951 Plymouth two-door sedan and a 1955 Dodge four-door sedan seems to be okay. Except the cars that is! Safety tip: When motoring in your vintage MoPar, take it slow and easy. (The Randy Fleischhauer Collection)

Here's one accident that probably took some doing to undo. The auto transporter was delivering two brand new 1957 Chevys when it ran into a ditch trying to avoid a 1955 Pontiac sedan in the snow. The car on top of the truck is a Chevy six, while the bottom deck holds another '57 Chevy with V-8 power. Go slow in the snow! (James W. Seymour photo from the Randy Fleischhauer Collection)

A tree limb knocked down in a storm damaged the hood, fender and windshield of this 1957 Chevrolet Bel Air Sports Sedan in 1988. The car, owned by a Wisconsin collector, has since been completely repaired. The photo underlines our advice that it's not a good idea to leave collector cars outside when heavy storm warnings are issued.

An open cab fire engine demolished a parked 1957 Oldsmobile 98, pushing it into a 1956 Cadillac 62 sedan in this California incident. The wreck took place in the early 1960s, not far from Los Angeles. (Courtesy National Motor Museum of Great Britain, Beaulieu, Hants, England)

This 1958 accident involved a Ford and a Buick. The 1957 Fairlane 500 two-door Club Victoria hardtop was one of 183,202 made. The 1955 Roadmaster Riviera hardtop was a bit rarer, with production of 80,338 units. It's interesting that a 1957 Buick is parked in the foreground of Randy Fleschhauer's photo, while the police car in the background is another '57 Ford.

This fire truck appears to be one of five Mack C-125 triple combination trucks delivered to the Los Angeles, Calif. Fire Department in 1958. It must have been most new when it ran into a parked 1957 Oldsmobile. Photo courtesy National Motor Museum, Beaulieu, England.

An accident in Illinois during 1957 involved a brand new Buick Special two-door sedan (one of 23,180 built) and a 1952 Ford Customline Tudor Sedan (one of 175,762 built). Damage to the right side of the Ford indicates left side of Buick has some damage, too. (James W. Seymour photo from the Randy Fleischhauer Collection)

This chain reaction crash photo came from Michael E. Ware, curator of the National Motor Museum in Beaulieu, England. It was part of the Crummett Collection, purchased by the museum 14 years ago in the United States. The setting is California, but details about the wreck are unavailable. The damaged cars would have a total value of approximately $50,000 today, according to Krause Publication's **Old Cars Price Guide**.

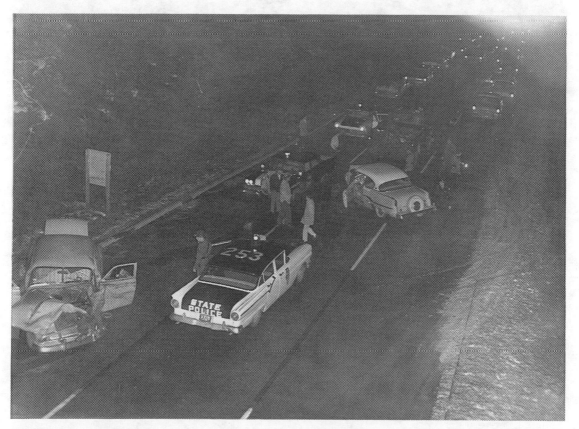

The aftermath of many motor vehicle accidents is a major traffic tie-up. That's what happened after these two cars collided, at night, on an Illinois highway. Note the 1957 Ford state police cars and the continental kit on the '54 Dodge which was damaged. (James W. Seymour photo courtesy of The Randy Fleischhauer Collection)

This fender-bender occurred on Broadway, but we don't know the name of the town, in northern Illinois, where it took place. The sun-visored 1950 Pontiac Chieftain Eight Deluxe sedan rammed into the side of the 1958 Chevrolet Biscayne two-door hardtop. Drive your postwar GM products carefully! (Randy Fleischhauer Collection)

It looks like someone got mad and "punched out the headlights" of this 1958 Chevrolet. The badge on the hood, below the Chevy emblem, reveals that it's a V-8 model. Check out the bald front tire. Postwar collector cars need good tires, too! (James W. Seymour photo from the Randy Fleischhauer Collection)

This photo of a wrecked 1958 Chevrolet police car came from the National Motor Museum of Great Britain. The patrolman behind the car's open passenger door looks a bit stressed, as he gets ready to fill out paperwork about the incident.

Two codes on the back of this old photo read "DI for ID; 5/3/67; J.G." and "P10 IE; 5/31/67; J.G." Apparently, the Dodge Coronet Royal Lancer had reached the tender age of nine-years-old, before it ran into an immovable object. The frontal damage is quite extensive. Drive your old Dodge safely!

Here is one of the 730 Cadillac Fleetwood Imperial limousines which were built in 1958 and it's a total wreck. If this limo looks small, the reason is that its body is bent in the middle. Make a "big" safety contribution — drive your old limos safely! (Photo by James W. Seymour courtesy The Randy Fleischhauer Collection)

The license plates indicates that this car was wrecked during 1965 in Illinois. In fact, the 1959 Impala Sport Sedan was sold by KB Chevrolet/Olds of Kankakee. Its retail value, at the time of the crash, was about $615. Careful driving will help keep your Impala in one piece! (James W. Seymour photo from the Randy Fleischhauer Collection)

This 1959 Ford was just a year old when it had a fender-bender. Photos like this one should make you think about adding "Lifeguard" safety features to 1956-1959 Fords undergoing restoration work. Such features were introduced by Ford in that era, but were not well-received by the buying public. Guard your life with safe driving of all your collector cars! (James W. Seymour photo from the Randy Fleischhauer Collection)

This beverage truck was used by a company in Springfield, Mo., until it was involved in an accident. It appears to be a Ford N-series model. These trucks used the same basic styling from 1963-1969. Commercial vehicle historian Professor Don Wood sent the picture, which might inspire the driving advice, "Say safety please!"

On Dec. 11, 1963, this three-year old Ford Ranch Wagon drove into a huge culvert during construction of Interstate Highway 80 near Kickersville, Ohio. The car, one of 43,872 built, appears to be a total wreck. Jim D. Jones, of Cincinnati, sent the photo as a reminder to drive cautiously in construction areas.

Of the many accident photos that Randy Fleischhauer, of Mesa, Ariz. has collected, this one of a wrecked 1960 Ford four-door sedan is special. He was driving it in 1962, when it crashed, and still has scars to show for it.

A Dodge ambulance was called to the scene of this accident, which involved a 1960 Ford Galaxie four-door sedan. The front of the car is completely wrecked, requiring a rather large tow truck for hauling it away. (The Randy Fleischhauer Collection)

It looks like someone tried to restyle this 1962 Plymouth Valiant by rolling it end-over-end several times. The accident occurred on July 19, 1962 on State Road 79 near Newark, Ohio. Jim D. Jones, of Cincinnati, took the picture. Plymouth collectors — don't let your car wind up like this — practice safe driving habits!

Ford built only 17,011 Falcon Futura coupes in 1962. This example survived only three years, before being banged-up in an accident that took place in the "Land of Lincoln." Drive your Falcon safely! (James W. Seymour photo from the Randy Fleischhauer Collection)

This 1963 Chevrolet Biscayne four-door station wagon sold for $2,830 with a V-8. The front fender badge indicates that this example had this type of powerplant. The sturdy wagon took a solid hit in its right rear quarter, but didn't even loose a wheel cover. Drive your postwar wagon carefully! (James W. Seymour photo from the Randy Fleischhauer Collection)